THE ADVENTURE SERIES

SCUBA-DIVING

ANNEKA RICE

Robson Books

Cartoons by Larry
Line drawings by Harold King

First published in Great Britain in 1988 by Robson Books Ltd,
Bolsover House, 5–6 Clipstone Street, London W1P 7EB.

British Library Cataloguing in Publication Data

Rice, Anneka
Scuba-diving – (The Adventure Series)
1. Scuba diving
I. Title II. Series
797.2'3 GV840.S78

ISBN 0-86051-463-3

Typeset by Rowland Phototypesetting Ltd,
Bury St Edmunds, Suffolk

Printed in Great Britain by St Edmundsbury Press Ltd,
Bury St Edmunds, Suffolk

Bound by Dorstel Press Ltd, Harlow, Essex

THE ADVENTURE SERIES

SCUBA-DIVING

THE ADVENTURE SERIES

Anneka Rice

SKIING

SAILING

Acknowledgements

Many people have helped me to learn to scuba-dive, and to put this book together. Ray Robinson and Alex Double were the photographers, and Nancy Duin did a great deal of additional research. I would also like to thank the crew of the *Lady Jenny V*, especially Alex, Adrian and Tamara for their help and hospitality both in and out of water.

Thanks to these – and to everyone else.

Foreword

Diving can be pure magic! Divers enter a world of weightlessness, colour and excitement, inhabited by strange animals and shapes, to explore underwater landscapes which form the last parts of our planet that are still unknown.

Diving is fun, too – once you have mastered the equipment and learned all the rules that you must follow to be safe. It is a sport that you share with others, and especially with the 'buddy' diver who is with you underwater.

It needs to be emphasized, however, that you *must* have proper training – not just from a book, but from a qualified instructor. At the London Underwater Centre (one of over 50 schools recognized by the British Sub-Aqua Club), we have taught more than 1000 beginners, ranging from 12- to 70-year-olds. Providing that you are in good health and can swim, diving could be for you.

Although I've been diving for more years than I care to remember, teaching Anneka – and being filmed doing it – was a new experience. Mike Portelly, who directed the film and also shot all the underwater footage, is generally acknowledged as the most creative underwater film-maker in the world. Although an old friend, in the Red Sea he was transformed into a demon director with an obsessive determination to get the right shot: I still remember how, on the seabed, his face contorted in fury as I misunderstood his signals yet again. At one point, I felt that the only adequate response would be to draw my diving knife and commit underwater hara-kiri! Nevertheless, his enthusiasm infected us all, and I know that, given the chance, every one of us would be back with him tomorrow. His film expresses better than any I've seen the beauty that is revealed to a beginner entering the sea for the first time.

Anneka herself was a wonderful pupil, always cheerful and responsive even when she was secretly worried, surviving close encounters with stonefish, lionfish, Napoleon wrasse and the nose of a certain instructor! In this book, she tells exactly how it feels to become a diver: the initial nervousness that turns into excitement, the *'après*-dive' satisfaction of achievement, the friendship and shared experiences. She's 'won her fins' now and can dive with the best of them.

Reg Vallintine
Chairman, BSAC Schools
Director, London Underwater Centre

DAY 1

Why did I choose sports for the Adventure Series which involve so much kit? Why didn't I decide to make a series about 'Nude Sunbathing in the Greek Islands' or 'Birdwatching on Wimbledon Common'? Instead, here I was surrounded by obscure, bulky pieces of equipment that looked as though they'd come out of the small ads of *Plumbing and Drainage Weekly*. How I'd get them on the plane, much less through the desert wastes of the Sinai peninsula, was a complete mystery to me.

It was a problem I'd have to solve because, today, we were flying to the Red Sea, where I would learn how to dive in what my instructor Reg Vallintine called 'the best classroom in the world'.

Reg and I have been friends for some time, but it had always been a source of disappointment to him that I wasn't also involved in the sport that had become the ruling passion of his life. I'd always said that I was simply too busy to spare the time, but finally I confessed that the idea of diving deep underwater chasing sharks wasn't high on my list of priorities. As it was, I spent most of my time dangling down potholes or hanging out of helicopters – who needed excitement?

Also, to tell the truth, the thought of being underwater with half a ton of equipment strapped on made me feel slightly claustrophobic. Reg told me that this wasn't unusual – in fact, according to him, most people quake at the thought – but there is a sensible way round this: pool training. In the secure confines of a pool,

Wet and dry suits

There are two reasons why I needed to wear something over my swimsuit: to keep warm (even in the tropics, the water can be significantly colder away from the surface); and to protect my skin, against scrapes and cuts, especially those caused by coral, and from the stings of a variety of sea creatures. Having tried on some diving

Day 1 continued

you can develop the confidence in yourself and your equipment that you'll need to enjoy diving in the open water. When I heard this, I was a little reassured, but the moment to learn had not yet arrived.

When we began discussing what we were going to include in the Adventure Series, learning to dive was a natural. Reg was obviously very pleased and more than willing to act as my instructor. And it was on his recommendation (and here we were undoubtedly influenced by his descriptions of the sheer magnificence of the waters of the Red Sea) that we were poised to fly to Eilat at the southern tip of Israel. I would be able to take my full novice diver's course with Reg – all the pool training, lectures and qualifying dives – in this divers' paradise. As it happens, Reg's old diving partner, Alex Double, and his wife Tamara conveniently run a British Sub-Aqua Club (BSAC) school in the Red Sea itself, on board a boat called the *Lady Jenny*. After the pool training in Eilat, what better place to complete my course?

equipment before, I knew how it would rub painfully against my skin if it weren't protected. Those glamorous underwater models, wearing nothing but their equipment and a brief excuse for a swimsuit, sacrifice a great deal for their art!

You can choose between wet suits and dry suits. *Wet suits* come in four pieces: trousers or, alternatively, long johns that come up over the shoulders; a jacket; a hood, either separate from or attached to the jacket (the latter is much warmer); and bootees. They are made of expanded foam neoprene, which contains thousands of nitrogen bubbles. Because of the pressure of water, the buoyancy characteristics of the suit will change as you go down. On the surface, you'll be very buoyant and have to wear extra weight to counteract this, but as you

Day 1 continued

Accumulating all my equipment took some doing. Luckily, I already had a wet suit – considering all the times that I'd been immersed during the filming of various television programmes, it had been a sensible investment. I could also wear it for all kinds of watersports – for example, water skiing and windsurfing – as well as for diving.

It is quite common for diving schools to provide equipment for their beginners, and Reg was going to lend me almost everything. However, he told me that there were three relatively inexpensive items that it might be a good idea to buy for myself: my mask, fins and snorkel.

I could see the point of the first two, but a snorkel seemed a rather redundant prop for a diving holiday. However, according to Reg, they're used by divers when they come up to the surface far from their boat or from the shore and don't have enough air left in their cylinders to swim back underwater. If you have to swim on the surface wearing all your gear, it's far more comfortable and much less tiring to do so with your face always under the water, without having to come up for air from time to time.

On Reg's advice, I headed for a proper dive shop, one that knew about divers' specific requirements.

Selecting the face mask came first. Human eyes are designed to see in air; everything looks fuzzy if you open your eyes underwater. However, if you put a layer of air between you and the briny deep, things improve – hence the mask. I was given a selection to try on, and then instructions on how to decide which one fitted best.

First, I had to place the mask over my eyes and nose without fastening the strap around my head. Then I had to breathe in through my nose and hold my breath. If the mask was a good fit, I should be able to tilt my head down without its falling off –

go deeper, the pressure compresses the material, you get heavier and some of the insulation is lost.

This loss will be somewhat compensated by the warmth provided by the thin layer of water trapped between your skin and the suit – hence the name *wet* suit. This water leaks in around the cuffs, waist, neck and ankles, and is then warmed by body heat. To be effective, the suit needs to fit tightly so that the water doesn't get flushed out again immediately to be replaced by cold water.

Wet suits come in thicknesses of 3 mm upwards. The thinnest are ideal for windsurfers, canoeists, water skiers and others who don't plan on spending much time in the water or who are only going to dive in shallow, warm water; alternatively, you can wear a shorty suit, or pool suit, which

Day 1 continued

Silicone masks are more expensive than rubber masks, but they should last longer. In addition, because they are translucent, you will be more aware of movement to the sides, outside your actual range of vision.

Before the mask is used for the first time, the face plate needs to be cleaned thoroughly to remove the silicon film which, if left on, will cause it to mist up. Household cleansers may help here.

that is, the suction should keep it on. If it was a bad fit, air would get in around the sides and the mask would fall off (in the sea, water would flood in).

I tried on quite a few masks and, in an expansive mood, decided to get two: a white one and a pink one (I later regretted this, as you'll see). I was to find that they became very personal pieces of equipment. Because everyone's face is a different shape, it was very important that I knew my masks fitted *me* – it can be very uncomfortable to be 10 metres down with a leaky one that keeps filling with water.

Fins – or 'flippers', as the Americans call them – came next. According to the shop manager, divers never use their arms and hands for swimming underwater: they are fully occupied with picking things up, checking gauges and so on. Instead, all forward propulsion should come from the legs and the fins.

There are two types of fins. The shoe design has a solid heel part, and the blades are usually quite flexible and so are good for initial training in a pool. With the other type, the front part of your foot is inserted into a pocket and the fin is held in place by a strap that goes round your heel. These straps are adjustable so that the fins can be worn with or without bootees; bootees will protect your feet from the rubbing of the fins. The blades are larger and stiffer than those of the

only reaches halfway to the knees. (But beware: the shorter, sawn-off type does some pretty unseemly things to the fleshy parts of your thighs!) True divers never regard anything less than 5 mm as adequate and will wear suits of 6–8 mm in UK waters.

You can buy a wet suit 'off the peg', the price depending on the thickness. If you are really keen (*and* have the money), you could have one made to measure.

Especially if you are planning on doing most of your diving in British waters, which can be very cold, you might consider getting one of the much warmer *dry suits*. There are two types, both of which are more expensive than wet suits.

The *neoprene dry suit* is made of the same material as the wet suit and

Day 1 continued

shoe type, so are more suitable for the open water. I selected a pair of these.

I then chose my last piece of basic equipment: a snorkel. I made sure that the one I bought had a strap on the side to hold it securely in place until needed, but you can also buy ones with attached cords that you can hang round your neck. I bought a snorkel that had a slightly longer tube than some of the others on offer so that, if I dived in rough seas, it wouldn't get swamped.

My final purchase was a bit of an afterthought. I'd never bothered to buy neoprene bootees to make my wet suit complete; somehow, I'd never felt the need when swanning in front of the camera in Cyprus or wherever. However, now I remembered Reg telling me that, among the other delights of the Red Sea, there were lots of sea creatures with barbed and/or poisonous spines and lots of needle-sharp coral. So rather than needing the bootees to protect myself from the cold, I bought them to keep anything that could harm me at least a few millimetres away.

My next stop was the London Underwater Centre in west London where Reg teaches. He led me to a room which, frankly, resembled a medieval torture chamber! Hanging from the walls were all sorts of strange gadgets, harnesses, metal cylinders, rubbery jackets, trousers and boots, halters and waistcoats with hoses dangling off them; and on the floor were crates of masks and fins in a multitude of different sizes, colours and makes, and stacks of lead weights. Above all, there was a pervading smell of damp rubber.

He gestured towards the air cylinders. 'We won't be able to take these with us – because of airline regulations, they're not usually allowed on planes. Besides, because they weigh so much even when they're empty, you'd blow your baggage allowance immediately! The diving

In 1976, yoga expert Jacques Mayol set a depth record for diving without an aqualung when he dropped to 100 metres.

is very warm. The *membrane suit*, on the other hand, is like jumping into a body-shaped plastic bag sealed, like the neoprene dry suit, at the wrists and neck. Since it is so thin, you have to wear something underneath to keep you warm. Usually this will be a polyester acrylic undersuit known to the diving fraternity as the 'woolly bear', but you could try to emulate James Bond who, in one film, pulled

centre at Eilat will provide us all with cylinders and weight belts.'

He picked up a complicated-looking metal contraption with various hoses coming off it, each ending with another metal bit. I saw that one of these last also had a mouthpiece so I guessed it must be what I would breathe through, but I couldn't imagine how it would be connected to the air cylinder.

'This is a demand valve,' said Reg in response to the baffled look on my face. 'You'll be using it to take in the compressed air from the cylinder. Take it with you now; I'll explain how it works when we begin our training.' He then held up a round instrument with numbers on its face, connected to the demand valve by a narrow tube. 'That's also when I'll tell you about this contents

on a membrane suit over a dinner jacket and black tie. After a few unbelievable feats of aquatic derring-do, he left the water, cast aside his dry suit and emerged as the impeccable spy we all know and love! Our intrepid director, Mike Portelly, revelled in the glories of *his* dry suit.

Both types of dry suit can pose buoyancy problems, as the air trapped inside them will compress and expand depending on the depth. Because of this, these suits incorporate inflation and vent valves, and you need to have special training to learn how to overcome any problems.

I was going to have enough training to cope with just learning how to dive, so I stuck with my own wet suit. A little water never hurt anyone . . .

gauge as well as—' he gestured towards a table covered with what looked like bulky watches— 'depth gauges, diving watches and dive timers.'

We moved over to another part of the room where a variety of life jackets were hanging. 'When you're underwater, you'll have to be in control of your buoyancy – to be able to rise and descend at will. A simple surface life jacket, the kind you'd wear on a boat, will support you adequately on top of the water, but because there's only enough gas to fill it at surface pressure, it won't be able to lift you from any depth. What you need is an adjustable buoyancy life jacket: an ABLJ, for short. This is directly connected to your air cylinder so that you can let in air to make you rise.'

There were two sorts of life jackets hanging on the wall: halters that you had to put on over your head, and a waistcoat type incorporating a ring on the back to hook the

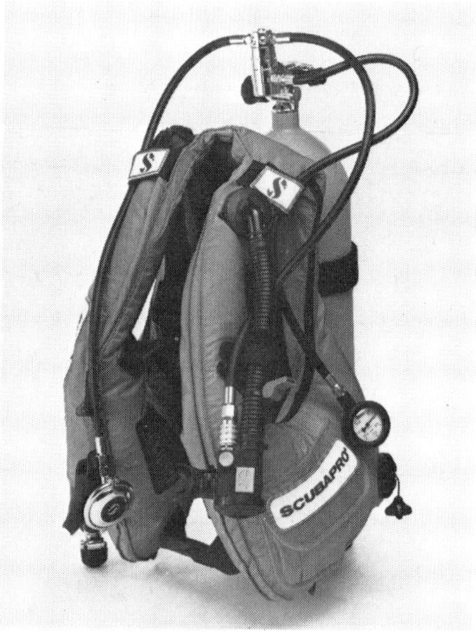

cylinder on. I tried on a few of both kinds, and then Reg suggested that I choose one of the waistcoats, a variety called a 'stab' (for 'stabilizer') jacket, because it would keep the air lower down, around my middle.

'Whether you're borrowing, renting or buying your equipment,' he continued, 'you should always try

The Diver's Code of Conduct

More and more people are taking to the water – some for recreation, some to earn their living. This code (devised by the British Sub-Aqua Club) is designed to ensure that divers do not come into conflict with other water users. It is vital that you observe it at all times.

Before leaving home

Contact the nearest BSAC branch or the dive operator local to the dive site. Seek advice from them about the local conditions and regulations.

On the beach, riverbank or lakeside

1 Obtain permission before diving

out at least a few of each thing before deciding: bad or uncomfortable equipment can lead to unnecessary problems underwater. You should also remember to check that everything you get is compatible with your other equipment.'

Now we turned to a selection of deadly looking knives. I had a sudden vision of Reg and me, each with a patch over one eye, leaping from a pirate ship, knives gripped between our teeth . . . Reg soon brought me back to reality.

'All divers need a knife – it's not for protection against attacks by beasties, but to free themselves from seaweed or fishing nets. Fishermen trawl near wrecks – favourite diving spots – because that's where fish gather, and consequently, a lot of discarded ropes and nets are found near them. If visibility is poor, it's easy to swim into seaweed or nets (some of which are virtually transparent underwater) and become entangled.'

He selected a knife. 'Here, this is a good one; it's got a very sharp serrated cutting edge.'

I handled it gingerly before slipping it into its carrier and placing it in my bag.

Reg continued his tour: 'Here are a couple of other things that are useful to have, but not absolutely essential for a beginner: a compass and a waterproof, rechargeable torch. It's easy to lose your way underwater, when there's no sun or landmarks to guide you. However, a diving compass, which you wear on your forearm, is really only effective if you read it with the arm bent in front of you at a constant angle: if you don't, it's all too easy to swim in a diagonal direction and go off course.

'You need a torch for night dives and when there's reduced visibility, such as in murky waters or in wrecks and caves. In addition, fish and coral tend to turn grey the deeper you go, but you can bring

in a harbour or estuary or in private water. Thank those responsible before you leave. Pay harbour dues.

2 Try to avoid overcrowding in one place. Consider other people on the beach.

3 Park sensibly. Avoid obstructing narrow approach roads. Keep off verges. Pay parking fees and use proper carparks.

4 Don't spread yourselves and your equipment since you may upset other people. Keep launching ramps and slipways clear.

5 Please keep the peace. Don't operate a compressor within earshot of other people – or late at night.

6 Pick up litter. Close gates. Be careful about fires. Avoid any damage to land or crops.

7 Obey special instructions such as National Trust rules, local by-laws and regulations about camping and caravanning.

Day 1 continued

their colours back by shining a torch on them.'

As I struggled to get everything Reg had lent me into my car, I wondered whether I'd ever be able to carry all this, let alone learn how to use it properly. I knew that Reg was a wonderful teacher, but was I an equally wonderful pupil?

Now I was faced with getting all this gear – fins, two masks, snorkel, 'stab' jacket, demand valve, knife and bootees, plus my wet suit and some books on diving Reg had given me and a few others on the flora and fauna of the Red Sea – into something that wouldn't take up the entire hold of the plane! Somehow I managed to stow everything into a huge nylon holdall. Luckily, I didn't have much other baggage – mainly just swimsuits, shorts, T-shirts and flip-flops.

We had to get to Gatwick early for our flight to Eilat – with all our camera equipment, it was going to take a long time for us to get through the extremely comprehensive security check that the airline insists upon. Eventually, the team was assembled at the check-in. There were seven of us, including Graham Berry, the cameraman who works with me on *Treasure Hunt*; Ray Robinson, my good friend and stills photographer; director and underwater cameraman Mike Portelly, and, last but certainly not least, Reg.

I immediately fell foul of the famous security check. The burly security man, who had unpacked in a second what it had taken me two hours to pack that morning, triumphantly produced the knife he'd spotted as my bag slid through the X-ray machine. It was duly confiscated (I should have known better than to have kept it in my hand luggage), and I skulked off, feeling like a mugger on the run from Borstal. I never did see that knife again . . .

To my horror, the departure

8 Remember: divers in wet suits are conspicuous, and bad behaviour could ban us from beaches.

In and on the water

1 Mark your diving boats so that your Club can be identified easily. Unmarked boats may become suspect.

2 Ask the harbour-master or local officials where to launch your boat – and do as they say. Tell the Coastguard, or another responsible person, where you are going and tell them when you get back.

3 Stay away from buoys, pots and pot markers. Ask local fishermen where not to dive. Offer to help them recover lost gear.

4 Remember: ships have not got brakes, so avoid diving in fairways or areas of heavy surface traffic, and observe the *International Regula-*

lounge was filled with film crews: it looked like the BBC canteen! Memories of a trip to the Seychelles for *Wish You Were Here* flooded back. We'd wanted to portray the islands as a lovely, untouched paradise, but hadn't reckoned on all the British film crews we came across at every turn, among them one making the film *Castaway* and another making a drama for Yorkshire Television. It became a race against time to get a shot of me against the background of an empty, white beach before a jeep full of technicians turned up at the other end and set up in the middle of our picture! Now, at Gatwick, I had a horrible feeling that we were going to be pursued down the Sinai peninsula by cameramen intent on filming a remake of *Lawrence of Arabia*!

The plane left on time, and we settled down for the flight to Eilat. My diving holiday was to involve practical training – familiarization with equipment, supervised diving, learning how to rescue someone, etc. – and lectures on diving theory. As well as important lectures on all the bad things that can occur underwater such as decompression sickness and burst lung (who *does* their PR?), there was also one designed to make divers aware of the general history of their new sport. So, while we had time to kill, Reg took me back to the 17th century and Edmund Halley (of comet fame) and his diving bell . . .

The word 'snorkel' is derived from the German *schnorchel* – the name of the pipe used to ventilate World War II U-boats when they were submerged.

About four hours after leaving London, we landed at Eilat, and what with the difference in time zones, it was late by the time we got to the hotel.

We'd left one modern airport only to arrive at another, and then travelled to the King Solomon's

tions for the Prevention of Collisions at Sea.

5 Always fly the diving flag when diving, but not when on the way to, or from, the dive site. Never leave a boat unattended.

6 Do not come in to bathing beaches under power. Use any special approach lanes. Do not disturb any seal or bird colonies with your boats. Watch your wash in crowded anchorages.

7 Whenever possible, divers should use a surface marker buoy.

On conservation

1 Never use a speargun with an aqualung. Never use a speargun in freshwater.

2 Shellfish, such as crabs and lobsters, take several years to grow to maturity; over-collecting in an area soon depletes stocks. Only take ma-

Palace, a luxury hotel that could as easily have been in Miami Beach or on the Costa Brava. In fact, the name of good King Solomon (it's said that he built his port of Ezion-geber in the area) was the only clue that we were in the Holy Land.

Just as I was sinking into a deep sleep, a little note was pushed under my door. It was from our director, and said: 'Sleep well. See you tomorrow morning at 6.00 a.m. prompt. Mike.' Was this the shape of things to come . . .?

ture fish or shellfish and then only what you need for yourself. Never sell your catch or clean it in public or on the beach. Don't display your trophies.

3 Be conservation conscious. Avoid damage to seaweeds and the sea-bed. Do not bring up seafans, corals, starfish or sea urchins – in one moment, you can destroy years of growth.

4 Take photographs and notes – not specimens. Shoot with a camera, not a speargun – spearfishing makes fish shy of divers. Never spearfish wrasse or other inshore species since, once an area is depleted of such fish, it may take an extremely long time for them to recolonize.

On wrecks

1 Do not dive on a designated wreck site. These are indicated on Admiralty

Day 1 continued

Charts and marked by buoys or warning notices on the shore nearby.

2 Do not lift anything that appears to be of historical importance.

3 If you do discover a wreck, do not talk about it. Pinpoint the site, do a rough survey and report it to the BSAC Archaeology Adviser and the Council for Nautical Archaeology, who will advise you.

4 If you do not lift anything from the wreck, it is not necessary to report your discovery to the Receiver of Wrecks. If you do lift, you must report.

5 If your find is important, you may apply for it to be designated a protected site. Then you can build up a well-qualified team with the right credentials and proceed with a systematic survey or excavation under licence without outside interference.

DON'T LET DIVERS DOWN – KEEP TO THE DIVER'S CODE

Day 1 continued

From bells to freedom

People have been diving for thousands of years. In the early days, divers would devise their own equipment and use it until the day they invariably came to a sticky end, primarily because they hadn't any idea about the laws of pressure. Breathing through a tube attached to the surface doesn't work at depths of more than half a metre: the extra water pressure on the chest prevents the breathing muscles from working.

The first apparatus designed for use by other people was probably the diving bell – a glorified upturned bucket lowered carefully into the water so that air was trapped inside. As the bell descended, the air would become compressed by the pressure of the water. Divers would stand underneath the bell, breathe in a lungful and then pop out and do whatever they had to do – salvage work, repair work and so on.

The problem was, the air would soon be used up. In addition, the divers would also breathe *out* waste carbon dioxide into the bell, making an unhealthy mixture of the air that remained.

In 1690, a more effective method was designed by Edmund Halley of Halley's Comet fame. His idea was to send down barrels of air to keep the air supply fresh. Outside the bell, the divers breathed this air fed to them through umbilical cords, and so they were able to stay down longer and undertake more complex tasks. This arrangement was fine as long as they didn't try to go any deeper than the depth of the bell; if they did, the increased pressure of the water would hamper their breathing.

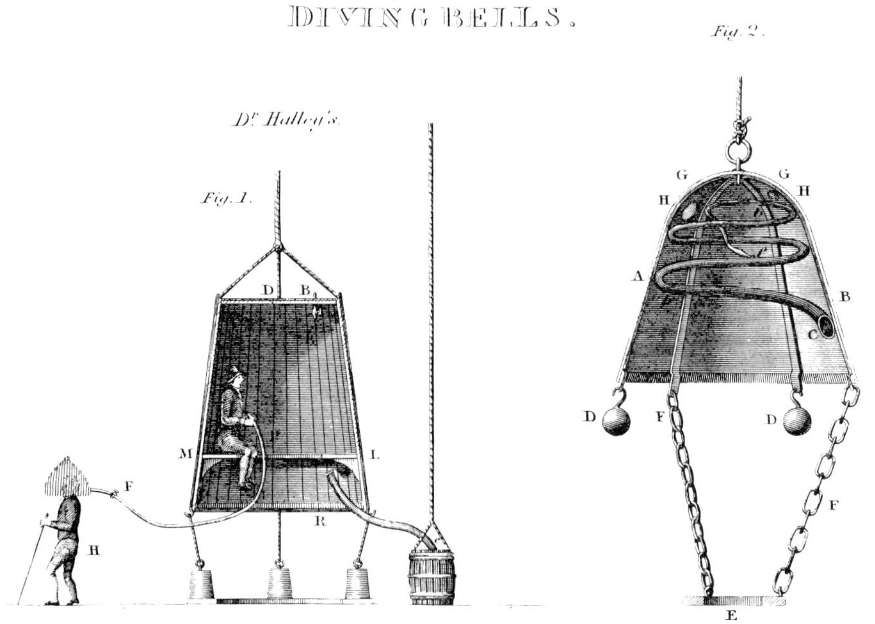

Day 1 continued

Halley's bell proved to be one of the most successful inventions of the time, divers (among them Halley himself) recording stays of up to 1½ hours at depths of over 16 metres.

A quarter of a century later, John Lethbridge of Newton Abbot produced another device that, rather surprisingly, worked quite well, too. Perhaps it simply had to: Lethbridge had 17 children to support, and he needed to have his wits about him to earn enough to keep the wolf from the door!

His invention was basically a wooden tube closed at each end, in which he lay horizontally, viewing the world through a small window in the side. While still on the surface, the tube was pumped full of air by means of a bellows, and then an assistant would lower it into the water, sometimes to a depth of 18 metres, where the Devon man would work with his arms sticking out of holes in the same side as the viewing window. Lethbridge was hired to recover gold bars from wrecked ships owned by the Dutch East India Company, and his only complaint was the effect of the increasing pressure on his arms, which were, of course, at a different pressure than the rest of his body.

All these early, imaginative designs led to the invention of the classic deep-sea helmeted diver's suit, which was only really abandoned about 20 years ago. The diving helmet itself had a curious birth – in a burning stable in Whitstable in about 1820.

A team of horses was trapped inside, but the dense smoke made it seemingly impossible to rescue them. However, watching the blaze was a local man who suddenly had an idea. John Deane ran to borrow a helmet from a suit of armour in the farmhouse and, on the way back, unhooked a pump from its water supply. He then attached a hose to the pump outlet, and secured the other end to the inside of the helmet. He asked someone to pump slowly, and wearing the air-filled helmet, entered the burning barn and, one at a time, brought out all the horses.

Deane's brother Charles patented the idea for fire-fighting, but the more imaginative John saw its potential for diving. He worked out a system

Day 1 continued

whereby air would be pumped into the helmet by two men on the surface operating a wheel pump (later replaced by a compressor), combined the helmet with a watertight suit and was ready to carry out undersea work – or so he thought. When he first tried out the suit in the sea, he found that air inflated the suit, the heavy copper helmet plunged down and his body flew up! His solution: a pair of lead boots to keep him upright.

The two brothers went into business as salvage engineers, charging the then enormous fee of five guineas a day. Among other commissions, they were involved in the building of the Houses of Parliament, laying the piles for its base in the Thames, and worked on the wreck of the *Mary Rose* in the Solent, about 150 years before Prince Charles got his chance.

The next big advance for divers came in 1865 when two Frenchmen – August Denayrouze of the French Navy and engineer Benoit Rouquayrol – produced the *aerophore*, which incorporated a cylinder of compressed air. However, the most important feature of their design was a primitive demand valve, which semi-automatically supplied air to divers at the same pressure as the water around them. They were, in effect, giving divers the freedom of the seas, who now were no longer restricted to one area by the umbilical cord of their air supply. (Jules Verne equipped Captain Nemo's men with an 'improved' version of the aerophore!)

With this new freedom, diving began to appeal to the general public, and eventually the first diving club was set up in Paris in 1930. Here, to the wonderment of onlookers, plimsoll-shod divers walked about on the bottom of a tank, clutching cylinders of air to their chests . . .

During World War II, diving received a big boost in public perception when frogmen became famous for their daring exploits. Instead of air – which is a combination of 78 per cent nitrogen and 21 per cent oxygen, the remaining 1 per cent being traces of carbon dioxide, argon and other gases – they used an enclosed system of pure oxygen. Because they didn't produce any bubbles, they were able to dive undetected to carry out sabotage, and even today, some underwater photographers use the same system so that bubbles don't ruin their shots. Breathing pure oxygen is, however, very different from using compressed air, mainly because oxygen becomes poisonous at depths below 10 metres, and specialized training is necessary. Frogmen also popularized the use of fins – invented by De Corlieu, a French commandant.

In 1943, another French naval

officer, Jacques-Yves Cousteau, joined forces with a Parisian engineer, Émile Gagnan, to produce the aqualung – or, as the Americans call it, the 'self-contained underwater breathing apparatus', or SCUBA. Gagnan had been trying to work out a way of feeding cooking gas into cars, to overcome the wartime scarcity of petrol. After hearing Cousteau's requirements, he adapted his design and the result was a fully-fledged demand valve, which provided divers with air, not continuously, but only when they inhaled, and expelled foul air directly into the water. As Cousteau has said, 'The sport was born.'

In the United States, there are now millions of people involved in diving. The popularity of the sport there has a lot to do with the fact that Cousteau sold a great deal of equipment in America, becoming quite famous along the way, especially through his television series *The Undersea World of Jacques Cousteau*.

In Britain, sport shops were reluctant to sell aqualungs because of scare stories about burst lung and the bends. As a result, the Underwater Explorers Club and the British Sub-Aqua Club (BSAC) were formed in 1953, and both were based at swimming pools because that seemed the most sensible place for people to start learning. Since then, about 400,000 people have been trained or registered by the BSAC, and today it has approximately 35,000 members, making it the largest diving club in the world with over 1000 branches at home and abroad.

As a fully trained diver, a whole new world is open to you – one of miraculous sights, exciting discoveries and engrossing activities such as archaeology and underwater photography and film-making. You can dive around the coasts of Britain or in inland waters, but you also have the seas of the world to explore if you feel the urge to travel . . .

DAY 2

When my alarm rang at 5.30 a.m., I leapt out of bed in a panic, not wanting to be late for the first day's filming. As I opened the curtains, an extraordinary sight greeted me. In one direction, the seemingly lifeless Negev desert; in the other, a sparkling resort. It was exactly like an oasis: nothing, nothing and nothing and then suddenly a cluster of luxury hotels.

Eilat's setting is stunning. Behind it loom the sandstone-and-granite mountains of the Sinai, and when the rays of the setting sun hit these and the mountains of biblical Edom which squat behind Aqaba in neighbouring Jordan, they are transformed into magical peaks of red and pink. These colours are, in turn, reflected in the normally brilliant blue waters of the Red Sea – providing at least one theory for the name. (Another is that it is a corruption of 'Reed Sea'.)

For a place of such biblical origins, it comes as quite a shock to see this modern city of 20,000, crowded with gleaming white buildings and buzzing with a feeling of 'anything goes'. In fact, in the 1970s it was a haven for hippies, and the atmosphere is still freewheeling.

Although Eilat is really just another man-made resort, its creation must have taken a great deal of determination, considering how unforgiving the arid Negev is. In 1949, the place comprised only three mud huts; now it's a major tourist centre, attracting (among others) divers from all over the world.

I finally unpacked, trying to untangle my wet suit from my fins and

During his experiments on pressure in the 17th century – which resulted in his 'Law' (that gas pressure and volume are inversely proportional at constant temperature) – the Anglo-Irish scientist Robert Boyle noted that a tiny bubble had appeared in the eye of a viper that he had placed in a pressure chamber and then decompressed. Unfortunately for divers, he neglected to link the importance of this effect with decompression sickness, or 'the bends', and they had to wait another 200 years for it to be fully understood.

Day 2 continued

Reg Vallintine

The aqualung

To dive safely, you need a method of breathing that will give you air at the same pressure as the water surrounding you, and one that will give you this *on demand* – that is, every time you inhale. There must also be a way of ridding the body of carbon dioxide, the waste product in used air, and the apparatus must be easy to carry on the body.

For hundreds of years, many inventive minds worked on this problem, but it wasn't until 1943 that Jacques-Yves Cousteau and Émile Gagnan produced what came to be called the *aqualung*. Although this 'breathing machine' has been greatly improved since then, the basic principles remain the same.

The aqualung comes in two main

Day 2 continued

Always get on the right side of your director

masks. When I'd finished, I put on my swimsuit and lugged all my diving things down to the poolside. Reg was already there, surrounded by a dejected film crew and piles of equipment.

Mike was looking accusingly at the sky: at 6.00 a.m. the pool was still in shadow. The filming was postponed. While our director tore his hair out, the rest of us tucked into what we didn't realize then was going to be our last proper breakfast for the whole trip! By 9.30, the sun had hit the pool and we were in business.

Reg and I were summoned to the poolside. Although only about my height, Reg is quite a big man – I

parts: the cylinder and the demand valve (or regulator).

The cylinder

A cylinder can vary greatly in size and shape, and is made of either aluminium or a steel alloy. It's the heaviest piece of diving equipment, but this weight becomes far less underwater.

The cylinder contains air that's compressed to a high pressure – usually about 200 bars (1 bar = 1 atmosphere) – which makes it possible to carry a great deal more air than if it were at a normal pressure. The cylinder is 'charged' with air by a high-pressure compressor, and its size and working pressure and how much it weighs will be noted on the cylinder itself, as will be the dates when it was tested and the test pressure.

Day 2 continued

mean, we are talking *big* here. Because of his outdoor life, he always looks incredibly healthy and, with his curly white hair and trimmed beard, very distinguished. He's an extremely experienced instructor, one of the most experienced in Britain; in fact, all the books on diving that I'd studied before this trip had been written by him. Knowing that someone like Reg would be in charge of my training was very comforting.

He'd already checked out my swimming, snorkelling and finning ability before we left London, so we could now concentrate on the intricacies of the aqualung.

'Before you get into your wet suit, let's talk about your equipment,' Reg said with a reassuring smile.

I then listened while he explained how my 'stab' jacket was connected to the cylinder of compressed air so that I could let air in and out to control my buoyancy.

'This is the demand valve, or regulator,' he continued, showing me a circular instrument with an attached mouthpiece. 'This will give you the air you need underwater. Why don't you try breathing through it now?'

'This way up?' I asked, as I pushed a button and air blasted into my face.

The amount of air a cylinder contains will determine how long you can dive, although this will also depend on how deep you go. A single cylinder's worth is usually enough for most divers, but more advanced divers who wish to go deeper and stay down longer can use twin cylinders.

Most well-run diving centres will refuse to rent cylinders to or fill empty ones for people who aren't qualified divers. Thus you should always remember to take along your qualification record, or you should go with your instructor.

The demand valve (regulator)

When air is compressed to 200 bars,

Day 2 continued

'That way.'

I put it in my mouth so that it fitted like the gumshield of an American football player; it had a strange rubbery/salty taste. I inhaled tentatively and got a shot of air deep into my mouth.

'OK?' asked Reg, peering into my face. 'It's as simple as breathing through a snorkel, simpler in fact because you're not going to get water splashing down. The principle of the demand valve is that it gives you air at the same pressure as the water you're swimming through. So when you're deep down, you just breathe normally but you inhale much more air with each breath.'

As I took out the demand valve, he added, 'What you must *never* do is hold your breath when coming up. If you do, that air will expand in your lungs as the pressure lessens and you could suffer something called "burst lung".'

'A *burst* lung, literally? That's a bit drastic.'

'Well, it can be. It's one of the most dangerous things in diving, but I'll give you a whole lecture about it later. Just remember to keep breathing normally – or, in an emergency, if you have no air, let the air out as you come up, as though you were blowing it out whistling.'

'Is it too late to get out of this now?'

'Anneka, you're going to love it!'

I wasn't too sure about that. Mastering this technology was going to be a weighty responsibility. I'm not the kind of person who likes to take *any* sort of life-or-death responsibility. It's the same when I go, say, abseiling or parachuting: I always want someone else to put the harness on me, so that if I fall, it will be *their* fault. (Yes, I do have a strange sense of justice . . .)

Reg then explained one of the basics of diving: you never dive

it's obviously under too high a pressure to be breathed directly, so there must be a mechanism between the air and the diver to allow the air to be used. This mechanism is the demand valve, also known as a regulator.

The demand valve comes in two stages. The first clamps directly on to the cylinder, and when air flows through this, it's reduced to about 10 bars above the surrounding atmospheric pressure. This air reaches the second stage of the demand valve via a hose.

The second stage is itself divided into two parts – a dry compartment and a compartment open to the water – which are separated by a flexible, pressure-sensitive diaphragm. The action of this causes any air that enters the dry compartment to become

Day 2 continued

alone. You always have a diving partner – a 'buddy' – who is your other pair of eyes, who will check your equipment and watch out for you. It was this kind of camaraderie that I was to find one of the most attractive aspects of the sport.

Now my 'buddy' Reg was urging me to join him in the water for the first time. I squeezed myself into my wet suit but left off the jacket for, even though it was only the end of April, it was already in the 80s. Then I had to put on the equipment.

Well, I'd always thought that diving equipment looked terribly glamorous when it was attached to Jacques Cousteau floating through

the same pressure as the water on the outside.

When the diver inhales through the mouthpiece, the suction causes the diaphragm to move inwards, opening up a valve in the dry compartment. This regulates the amount of air that enters the compartment, thus allowing the diver to breathe.

When the diver exhales, the rush of air pushes the diaphragm outwards. This causes another valve on the opposite side of the dry compartment to open and vent the used air.

In addition to the demand valve itself, there's a tap at the top of the cylinder to turn on and off the air supply. There's also a hose (called the 'direct feed') attached to the first stage of the demand valve, which will be connected to your life jacket; and a

Day 2 continued

the sea, collecting beautiful bright green fish and photographing rare marine life. Now I realized how heavy it all was: not only did the air cylinder weigh a ton, but I also had to wear a weight belt carrying a lot of extra kilograms to counteract the natural buoyancy of my body and my wet suit. Although Reg told me that I would lose all the weight when I got in, walking about beside the pool in my fins made me feel like a very clumsy and very heavy penguin.

'OK, Anneka, this is where the fun starts. That's right, backwards down the ladder like I did . . .'

Even though the sun was beating down on our backs, it was good to have the wet suit on: the equipment was heavy and uncomfortable against my skin.

'While your mask is dry, spit on the inside of the faceplate and then rinse it out – that will keep it from misting underwater.'

I did as Reg asked, thinking that, in comparison with the high tech of the other equipment, this was all a bit primitive.

'Put your mask on – that's right, brush your hair out of the way – mouthpiece in and just bend at the knees and put your face in the water so that you can try breathing.'

Almost all the divers that I'd talked to back home had mentioned

contents gauge (also attached by a hose to the first stage of the demand valve), which you'll have to monitor frequently to check how much air you have left.

Mask squeeze

As well as the airspaces within the body, the air contained in the space between your mask and your face can also be affected by changes in water pressure. If you should dive down suddenly or if you inadvertently breathe *in* through your nose, the air in the mask will drop in pressure and the mask will begin to squeeze un-

> ***Never* dive with earplugs. The external pressure of the water may push them too far into the ears, and even if they stay in place, air will be trapped between them and the eardrums. This air will remain at a lower pressure than that on the other side of the eardrums, and consequently, the eardrums may burst outwards–a serious condition known as 'reversed ear'.**

how daunting they'd found that first breath underwater, and I waited for an overwhelming feeling of claustrophobia. It never came: I took to underwater breathing like the proverbial duck to water. I felt fantastic – there I was, head down in the water and *breathing*!

To Reg's relief, I came up smiling. 'The system works! I can breathe underwater!'

'Great!' he replied, but we didn't stop to marvel at my transformation into an amphibian – there was too much still to learn.

'Now,' he said, 'just before we go into deeper water, I want to show you how to clear your ears. This is very important because the pressure on either side of your eardrums will be different, and you'll have to equalize it.

'To do this, you come up slightly, and then you could try swallowing or wiggling your jaw. If you're lucky, that may do the trick, but if you're like most people, you'll have to hold your nose through your mask and blow gently. This forces pressurized air up the Eustachian tube to your middle ear. Because you're more affected by pressure as you begin your descent, you need to do this ear-clearing constantly until you reach the desired depth.'

Reg demonstrated the technique and I imitated him. Even though I felt slightly ridiculous, I knew that it was vital. In the past, I'd been aware of an uncomfortable amount of pressure in my ears even when just diving into the deep end of a pool,

comfortably against your face.

This can be easily remedied if you blow some air *out* through your nose into the mask. However, if you continue a dive without doing this, the 'mask squeeze' can harm the blood vessels that lie under the skin and in the eyes. Usually, this will result in nothing more than bloodshot, black eyes – not a pretty sight, but one that will clear up in a few days – but it could lead to a more serious condition. So just as you check your ears as you descend, pay attention to the fit of your mask: if it becomes too tight, adjust the pressure within it by blowing out a little through your nose.

Day 2 continued

The ears and sinuses

Pressure can affect all the air spaces of the body, but unlike the lungs, which will contain compressed air, the ears and the sinuses have to be protected in a different way.

The ear has three parts. The outer ear is what we can see on the outside of the head, but it also includes the ear canal, sealed at one end by the eardrum. The middle ear, on the other side of the eardrum, is a cavity containing the tiny bones that are vital for the transfer of sound; it's also connected to the back of the nose by the Eustachian tube. Finally, there's the inner ear, where all the organs of balance are located.

You can also have trouble with your sinuses, the hollow spaces in the front of the head that are connected to the nasal cavity. You can equalize the pressure in them by blowing through your nose, just as you do for clearing your ears. But if the sinuses are blocked because you have a cold, the tissue in them will swell and bleed and you'll feel intense pain. The answer to this and to eardrum trouble is: *never* dive if you have a cold.

As you enter the water and then go deeper, water presses in on the eardrum; if this pressure isn't equalized on the other side – that is, through the Eustachian tube – the eardrum can be pushed inwards until it bursts. This isn't only extremely painful, it can seriously damage your hearing, and the water that rushes in can upset the balance organs so that you feel as if you're spinning around.

and that had been a lot shallower than the Red Sea would be!

'If you feel your ears hurting when you descend, come up a bit and try blowing again. No need to worry if someone is waiting for you. They'll understand.'

By now we had moved over to sit on the edge of the pool. I paddled my finned feet and tried to imagine what all this pressure could do to the inside of my head. Luckily Reg then turned his attention to a less painful subject.

'You obviously won't be able to talk underwater, so how will you be able to communicate with your buddy?' he asked rhetorically. 'You're in luck – you can use a set of hand signals that are understood around the world. The international ones come in three groups: your well-being or lack of it; air-supply signals; and direction signals.'

Reg showed me the two signals that we'd be using here in the pool. The first even I recognized: the 'OK'

If you run into trouble but your buddy is too far away to see your hand signals, you can alert him by banging your knife or a stone against your air cylinder. Sound travels five times faster in water than in air.

However, you should never use emergency cylinder banging for anything else – say, to call attention to a lovely piece of coral or an interesting fish.

SCUBAPRO

GUL

Hand signals

Underwater

GROUP 1:
YOUR WELL-BEING
OR LACK OF IT

OK

Both a question and an answer: 'Are you OK?' 'Yes.' Also means: 'Yes, I've understood that message.'

Something is wrong

Combine with other signals – e.g. 'Something is wrong', then point to ears, mask full of water, etc.

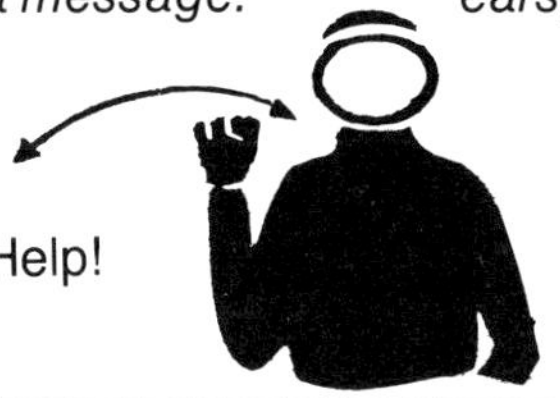

Help!

GROUP 2: AIR
SUPPLY SIGNALS

I am getting low on air

The dive leader will normally signal everybody to go up to surface.

I am out of air

Buddy should take action – e.g. shared breathing.

I am out of breath

If, for example, you're exhausted after a long swim, your companions should wait for you to get your breath back.

GROUP 3: DIRECTION SIGNALS

Let's go up

Not to be interpreted as 'OK'.

Let's go down

Let's go over there
or
You *or* me

Signals *on the surface*

OK

This should be acknowledged by someone on the boat.

Help!

The faster you wave, the more urgently you need help.

Day 2 continued

sign, a big clear circle formed by the forefinger and thumb. The second proved to be equally graphic: the 'unhappy' sign, which Reg nicknamed the 'dodgy Italian driver sign'. For this one, you rock your flat hand from side to side, as if trying to imitate the wing of a fluttering bird.

'Every time I give you the "OK" sign, Anneka, I want you to respond with a confident "OK" sign immediately afterwards. That's so I'll know that you're all right. And if anything is wrong, give me the "dodgy" sign as soon as possible.

'Always make your signals forcefully to emphasize them. If you do them in front of you, they may get lost against the background of your suit and equipment. If your buddy doesn't notice them, move closer.'

Following Reg's instructions, I began to swim around the pool, getting myself accustomed to the aqualung. Of course, he'd been right: once in the water, all the weight of the equipment disappeared as if by magic and I felt as light as a feather.

I'm a relatively good surface swimmer, and I think that's why I was able to swim with fins fairly well from the beginning. You have to fin with a strong, steady movement, with your legs slightly bent. If you keep your legs stiff, it's quite tiring, but if they're slightly bent it's easy and effective.

Satisfied with my progress, I swam up to Reg and surfaced with a smile. 'Now,' he said, 'we have to adjust your weight belt, so that you achieve what we call "neutral buoyancy" – that is, when you neither rise nor sink in the water. Lie face-down in the water. If you're correctly weighted, you should sink when you exhale and just start to rise when you inhale.'

When I did this, I stayed right on the top of the water, even when I exhaled, so I had to have more lead weights (about 6 kilograms' worth)

The teeth of the parrotfish are fused together so that its mouth resembles a beak. It uses this to bite off bits of coral to get at the polyps within as well as any other small animals that cling to the coral walls. The surprisingly loud sound of a parrotfish grazing among the coral is a familiar one to tropical divers.

Parrotfish are perfectly capable of digesting coral, being equipped with plate-like throat teeth that grind it up. The waste they expel is coral sand, and one fish can produce 5 tons of this in a year. In sufficient quantities, this pulverized limestone can change the shape of the seabed, and parrotfish have also been responsible for demolishing whole coral reefs.

added to my weight belt. Later, the fact that I needed *slightly* more weight than any of the others when dressed in my full wet suit – a total of 12 kilograms, in fact – became a standing joke. I kept trying to explain to the lads that women have natural in-built buoyancy!

When I'd finally achieved neutral buoyancy, I stood up in the pool. Reg warned me: 'Always put your weight belt on in such a way that, if you have to make an emergency ascent, you or your rescuer can get it off without any trouble.

'Now I want you to try removing your mouthpiece while you're underwater, so if it gets knocked out by accident, you won't panic.'

I obediently knelt on the bottom of the pool, took a breath like Reg had told me to, held it and then removed the mouthpiece. As it bubbled away in my hand, I did feel an inkling of panic even though Reg was right next to me – it was surprising how dependent I'd already be-

come on this artificial air supply. After a few seconds (which felt much longer), I replaced the mouthpiece and breathed *out*, to get rid of any water – now I could breathe normally. Then I returned to the surface.

'That was fine, Anneka,' Reg said. 'Now we'll deal with mask clearing. There are all kinds of

Giant clams, the largest of the molluscs, have played a prominent part in aquatic 'B' movies, but despite this, there is no record of any diver losing an arm or leg in a clam's toothless embrace. In fact, giant clams open and snap shut their shells because of a mechanism that works like a primitive electric eye. When the clam is open, certain cells in the shell admit light which falls on the animal's soft inner body; when the beam is interrupted by the presence of an object, the shell closes swiftly.

Giant clams have been known to produce pearls the size of golfballs. Unfortunately, these have no commercial value.

reasons why a mask can get water into it: a bad fit, a knock from some object or another diver or a fish. You have to learn how to flush out the water while you're still underwater, so you won't have to interrupt your dive, and for safety's sake, again to eliminate panic.

'Now, mask clearing is really very simple if you remember that what you're doing is replacing water with air. Go back into the water, lift the bottom rim of the mask and let some water in.'

I did as he requested. Although, before, I'd breathed quite happily through my mouth and hadn't even thought about my nose, now with it surrounded by water, I felt a great compulsion to breathe through it again. I straightened up and, spluttering, faced Reg with a nose full of water.

'Now,' he continued, 'press your fingers on the top rim and tilt your head back so that you're looking up, at what will be the surface. Then blow out through your nose. All the water will come out.'

I tried to remember how to sneeze, but whereas Reg could clear his mask easily in just one exhalation, it took me several snorts to clear mine.

'Now try it underwater,' said Reg.

Gulp, I thought, but down I went. It was a very weird feeling watching the water enter the mask, followed by that horrible compulsive feeling of wanting to sniff it all up. I did all right, but I must admit that I was never very happy with mask clearing. It was to remain my least favourite exercise for the rest of my Red Sea diving adventure.

After the mask clearing, the 'ditch-and-retrieve' drill was a doddle. This involved taking off my cylinder, mask and weight belt, leaving them on the bottom of the pool and surfacing. After gulping in a good lungful of air, I dived back down and, first grabbing the air supply and replacing the mouth-

Where to learn

By far the best places to learn how to dive are the schools recognized by the British Sub-Aqua Club. Here, nationally qualified instructors run introductory courses in pools, and teach novice and sport diver courses in open water, combining these with lectures on diving equipment and theory. There are about 20 BSAC diving schools dotted around Britain (inland and on coasts), as well as ones in Malta, Cyprus, the Cayman Islands and Gibraltar. You can learn full-time or take a class, say, once a week, either during the day or in the evening; alternatively, you can opt for private tuition. For more information, contact the BSAC, 16 Upper Woburn Place, London WC1H 0QW.

In addition, there are quite a number of diving centres around the world where courses recognized by the piece, put everything back on again.

Basically designed to build your confidence underwater, ditch-and-retrieve also makes you familiar with all the different straps that hold your equipment on. In addition, it prepares you for the extremely rare occasion when your cylinder might get stuck and you would have to remove it to continue on your way.

Air sharing came next – more emergencies! Reg explained: 'You may run out of air or have trouble with your demand valve so that air simply doesn't reach you. Obviously, you can't simply shoot to the surface – you could burst a lung that way – so you'll have to learn how to

World Underwater Federation can be taken. At these, you can learn how to dive in ideal conditions – in the Red Sea like I did or in the Caribbean, Mediterranean and Indian Ocean, all of which have warm, clear water with abundant marine life to gawp at! It is, however, probably a good idea to do your novice course in a swimming pool before leaving on holiday – that way, you can enjoy warm open-water diving as soon as you get there.

Even if you have achieved novice status before you go on holiday, you are still qualified to dive only with an instructor or an experienced dive guide – certainly not with divers who are at the same level as yourself or even lower. It is, therefore, very important to make sure before you go that those running your course or diving holiday have the necessary qualifications.

share air with your partner.

'Signal to him that you're having air-supply trouble, and when he gets to you, remove your mouthpiece. He'll pass you his mouthpiece, but he'll keep hold of it in case you panic – it's human nature to think only of yourself when your life is in danger! You breathe out through it first and then take a deep breath, exhale and then breathe in deeply once more, before passing the mouthpiece back. When you've established a good breathing rhythm, you'll be able to swim side by side together while making an ascent. Want to try it?'

We moved to the deep end of the pool and sank beneath the surface, clearing our ears all the way. Once on the bottom, Reg signalled to me to make the 'out of air' hand gesture – a karate chop to the throat – and take out my mouthpiece. Grasping Reg's jacket with one hand while he held on to the lifting handle of my air cylinder, we knelt on the bottom and passed his mouthpiece back and forth. Then we reversed our situations and he became the victim and I became the rescuer, finally swimming, still air sharing, to the surface.

What really struck me was the trust for Reg that I felt while underwater. I mean, he's a lovely man anyway and probably the best teacher anyone could ever have, but there's something about being able to communicate only with eyes and hands that creates a very strong bond. I must say, though, what with spitting in your mask and sharing mouthpieces, it certainly helps if you really like your instructor!

My brain seemed filled to the brim with equal measures of instructions and water. Reg reckoned that I'd had enough 'practical' for the first day, and told me to get dry and dressed for the afternoon's theory session.

Back in my hotel room, after I pulled off my wet suit and put on

Burst lung

We usually think of breathing as the movement of our lungs as we inhale and exhale. However, the parts of the body actually involved in the vital exchange of gases that constitutes breathing are the *alveoli* in the lungs. These are minute structures resembling clusters of grapes, covered with tiny blood vessels and located at the ends of the airways. Here the vessel walls are only one cell thick, and the oxygen you inhale passes through them into the general circulation, and waste carbon dioxide passes the other way to be exhaled.

Every breath of compressed air you inhale when you're diving contains much more air than it would on the surface – remember Boyle's Law? This will have no effect on your lungs

Day 2 continued

some dry clothes, I lay down for a while. I thought how lucky I was to be learning to dive here in the warm waters of the hotel pool and the sea, with the sun shining, drinks by the waterside, good friends – more of a holiday than anything else. And even when learning the basics, there would be amazing sights to marvel at in the Red Sea.

After lunch, Reg and I drove to Coral Beach, a short distance down the coast. This is a protected underwater park, complete with an underwater signposted trail for snorkellers, where you can spot

as long as you stay at the same depth. However, if you ascend and keep this air in your lungs by holding your breath, the lessening pressure will cause the air to expand, possibly leading to a serious condition that is commonly known as 'burst lung'.

The lungs themselves don't actually burst, but the walls of the alveoli do become stretched and may break, allowing air to escape into the bloodstream. This can have a number of consequences. The air can be trapped between the lungs and the chest wall – a condition called *pneumothorax* – and may cause a collapsed lung. It may also become trapped within the lung tissue (*emphysema*), or even under the skin. However, most serious of all is the possibility of an *air embolism*, when air in the bloodstream forms bubbles that such regulars of the coral reef as angel-, lion-, clown- and emperor fish – all in great profusion. Those who want to see this submarine world but remain dry can go on one of the glass-bottomed boats or on the semi-submersible trimaran. Alternatively, you can visit Coral World, which comprises a museum, aquariums and an underwater observatory, where Reg gave me my lecture on pressure.

One of only five in the world, the observatory is an amazing structure. Protruding 100 metres out to sea, its 20 large windows look out on a glorious profusion of coral and tropical marine life some 8 metres below the surface, and it was here that I had my first taste of the wonders that were in store for me.

But Reg and I had work to do, and so we tore our eyes away from the windows and turned our thoughts to the dangers of the deep.

'One of the interesting things about diving is how fast the pressure increases when you go down underwater,' he began. 'In this underwater observatory, the glass has to be an inch thick although we're only 8 metres underwater. When you go a little bit deeper, to 10 metres, the pressure increases by a whole "atmosphere" – that is, the weight of the air on the surface of the earth – so that you would be swimming in water at a pressure of 2 atmospheres (also expressed as 2 bars). Above the surface, we have to go to outer space to change it that much, to more or less a vacuum, but for every 10 metres underwater, the pressure increases by a whole atmosphere.

'Because we'll be wearing aqualungs, we won't feel this because, with the demand valve, the air in our lungs is kept at the same pressure as the sea, and as for the rest of our body, it's mostly made up of water which is virtually unaffected by pressure. But the old

travel round the circulation; one or more of these may block a vital artery and cause grave injury or even death.

The symptoms of burst lung are wide ranging: visual disturbance, confusion, nausea, weakness, dizziness, headache, paralysis, chest pain. Oddly enough, chest pain is not always apparent.

In air embolism, symptoms usually appear quite quickly – within 2 or 3 minutes – but it can be difficult to ascertain what exactly has happened. The best rule to follow is to take seriously any abnormal symptom that follows a rushed or otherwise abnormal ascent, and to make sure that the victim is taken back to the shore or ship immediately.

The victim should *not* be taken to a hospital but to a recompression chamber. These can be found at helmet divers had a *real* problem. If they slipped off a shallow reef and fell into the depths, the increasing pressure tended to ram the whole of their body up into the helmet, and it would, in extreme cases, come up the air tube, allegedly like tomato sauce. It was a pretty terrible way to die.'

'*Very* nice, Reg,' I said. 'So that's why you're always reminding me to keep clearing my ears the whole time?'

'Absolutely. If you didn't do that, the pressure would increase, the pain would increase and eventually you'd burst your eardrum.

'The other thing you need to know is about how volumes – the space that gases take up – change as the pressure changes. Imagine that we have an ordinary glass. If we turn it upside down and put the rim just through the surface of some very deep water, a whole glass full of air will be trapped inside, air that is at a pressure of 1 atmosphere.

'However, if we push the glass down under the water to a depth of 10 metres, we'll have doubled the pressure to 2 atmospheres. If we look in the glass, we'll find that we've got half the volume – in other words, the air has become compressed and the water has come up halfway. Actually, this is an example of a scientific principle known as Boyle's Law.'

Learning the theory side of diving

Known to the Arabs as the 'fish of death', the pink and purple lionfish (also called the dragon-, turkey- and zebrafish) is a thoroughly lovely denizen of the deep, with its large diaphanous fins and tail. However, this graceful animal can be deadly: on its back are 18 striped and spotted and extremely poisonous spines. Luckily, the dragonfish generally feeds on tiny crustaceans and other fishes, but it is capable of swallowing a victim almost as large as itself.

naval bases, major sport diving centres and elsewhere. (You should always find out where the nearest chamber is *before* diving.)

A recompression chamber is a large sealed cylinder in which there is a bed, intercom and observation window. Air is pumped into the chamber until it's at a higher pressure than the victim was when the abnormal ascent was made. With this increase in pressure, the air bubbles in the blood become smaller until they eventually disappear; then the pressure is very gradually returned to normal. A doctor will enter the chamber via a pressurized lock so that the victim's condition can be monitored. The shortest time that anyone suffering from burst lung would spend in a recompression chamber would be about 2½ hours, but you may have to stay was a bit like going back to school, but in such a nice environment, it wasn't such an onerous task. It did seem a lot to take in at one sitting, but I'd also been given some very good books to read later. Frankly, I was beginning to feel that only those with science degrees could possibly understand everything, but Reg did a great job of trying to make it simple enough to grasp, and in the end, I found it all fascinating.

Reg continued: 'The change in volume that occurs in air under pressure can badly affect the body if you don't breathe correctly, the worst situation being "burst lung". However, any compressed air that becomes trapped in the body and then expands on ascent will cause problems. For example, did you know that diving can give you a toothache?'

'No,' I replied hesitantly, not sure if he was joking.

'Well, it can. Sometimes decay

Like the air in your lungs when you hold your breath, any that you swallow into your stomach will expand as you ascend, and you may end up feeling like a baby with wind! This is not very serious as you can usually get rid of it with a good belch!

there for 24 hours or even longer.

Since burst lung can be so serious as to threaten life, it is important to do everything you can to avoid it. Usually, you simply breathe normally as you ascend, your demand valve ensuring that the air pressure decreases as you rise. However, if you have to return to the surface in an emergency because you've lost your air supply for some reason, you should breathe out slowly as you make your ascent, even though the natural reaction is to keep the last bit of air in your lungs for as long as possible. Alternatively, you can breathe some of your buddy's air, either by air sharing or by using his 'octopus rig' if he has one; this is an extra mouthpiece attached by a tube to his demand valve.

Day 2 continued

will create a small cavity where air can be trapped, or you may have badly fitting fillings with small pockets of air beneath them. There may be no way to equalize the air pressure in such air spaces and the result is toothache.

'I once went to my dentist and told him exactly which filling needed replacing. He was amazed to find that I was absolutely correct, and wondered how I could have known. "I'm a diver," I told him – and he dined out on that story for weeks!'

It was getting late, and even the fish outside the observatory windows seemed to be slowing down and getting ready for sleep. Reg called a halt to his lecture, and we made our way back to the hotel and dinner.

Despite all the heavy theory, I went to bed reassured. Of course, it isn't pleasant hearing about all the things that can go wrong, but as Reg had told me, you have to be pretty unlucky for an accident to happen. Diving is meant to be a sport, so while the instruction shouldn't be taken lightly, what you're doing should also be enjoyable. If you take all the safety precautions – and after practising them, they become second nature – you can get down to the serious fun that diving really is.

It was an inspired choice of Reg's to give me that lecture in the underwater observatory. Not only did it bring it all home to me, but it really whetted my appetite for my first dive.

I couldn't wait.

Many helmet divers who were badly affected by the bends believed that, from their first dives, they became divorced from life on land, where their awkwardness and pain gradually increased. With each successive dive, they were drawn more and more to the sea where, they thought, they were rewarded with a kind of elixir of youth, giving them painless mobility. What they were actually experiencing, of course, was the nitrogen bubbles becoming smaller so that they were forced back into solution in their blood.

DAY 3

I was woken by the ringing of the telephone. A sleepy receptionist informed me that it was 4.00 a.m. and Mike, our mad director, wanted the crew set up and ready to go in half an hour! I put down the phone, thinking it was some kind of practical joke . . . until there was a knock on the door and a cheery 'Come on, Anneka, let's get going!'

Except for Mad Mike, who never seemed to need sleep, the rest of us stumbled about in the half-light like a bunch of the walking dead. Graham looked as if he were in a state of shock. We climbed into the boat lent to us by the Red Sea Sports Club, one of several local diving centres, and about 20 minutes later, we were at the extraordinary Taba Beach on the east coast of the Sinai peninsula.

Mike tried to whip up enthusiasm as we gazed blankly at the dark horizon: 'Just you wait – this will be magnificent.'

Then, right on cue: *The dawn bled across the sky like a smear of orange paint on an indigo canvas* . . . That's what romantic novels tell us – they *don't* tell us how early it is! 'Isn't this incredible?' cried Mike as we sat there with matchsticks propping

In freshwater, you can drown in two minutes, but it can take up to ten in seawater. This is because seawater is much closer in consistency and salinity to our blood – a relic of our fishy past.

The fish of the reef

More than 1000 species of fish inhabit the coral reefs of the world, and many are extremely striking, displaying their vivid colours in stripes, spots, lozenges, dots and other markings. There is great variation, even among the same species, and some types change colour to reflect their age, sex, mood or the season, or to imitate other fish or their surroundings.

Day 3 continued

Why they come in so many colours and are often marked in such strange ways is still a mystery. There may be, however, not just one solution but a number. The function of some of the markings is to confuse predators. For example, on either side of its tail, the butterfly fish displays a large dark spot, ringed with white. The two spots resemble an extra pair of eyes, making any fish chasing it unsure of whether it is coming or going.

Other fish, such as the stonefish, have almost foolproof camouflage. Still others seem to court identification – the red, blue and white lionfish, for example, spreads its gauzy fans and shows its stings when threatened.

In addition, colours and markings identify members of the same species, but this works in two seemingly contradictory ways. First, it enables them to mate appropriately. How-

Day 3 continued

our eyes open, barely taking in our surroundings.

Before the 1967 Arab–Israeli war, Taba Beach and the rest of the Sinai were part of Egypt, but after the war, and for the following decade, this vast and mainly desolate territory was occupied by the Israelis. Then came the Camp David agreement, under which the Sinai was returned to the Egyptians. However, a few areas of dispute still remain, one of which is Taba Beach.

I wasn't going to get involved, and anyway, the Red Sea is a paradise for all divers, whatever nationality. We moored our boat at the jetty and waved to the Israeli guards stationed there with their machine guns. Reg, who has dived all over the world in virtually every situation imaginable, confessed that, even for him, a five o'clock start was a new one.

We dutifully got our gear ready. 'The waters here are ideal,' said Reg as he hoisted his cylinder on to his

back. 'They're shallow and safe and, as an added bonus, you'll get to see some of the scenery that attracts divers from all over the world.'

I was a bit dubious, although I didn't voice my thoughts. It's not that I didn't trust Reg; it was just

ever, reef fish are often extremely territorial, each member of a species making claim to a small section of the reef. If another member of the same species – identified by its colour and/or markings – strays into that area, the resident fish will defend its territory vigorously, but will leave other species (and divers) alone.

(Of course, none of these explanations answers the question of why there are vividly coloured reef fish inhabiting quite deep waters, where everything tends to fade into grey. Do these fish have a special ability to see colours that we don't?)

Almost all of the smaller fish are flat and round. This disc shape gives them great mobility, so that they can flee predators by hiding in tiny openings in the coral. They also have relatively short fins and large tails to enable them to turn quickly and pull up sharpish.

Day 3 continued

that, now I was in the open water, it seemed a lot more dangerous than diving in the confines of the hotel pool. At least there, if you got into trouble, you'd have someone only a few feet above you ready to lend a hand – even if it was just a member of the film crew. Now I really did have to depend on Reg.

As always, safety was foremost in Reg's mind, and now that we were all kitted out, it was time to see if we'd put on everything correctly.

'Right, we'll do our pre-dive check now, Anneka,' he said. 'Do you remember what you check?'

'Yes, your weight belt, to make sure I can get to it quickly.'

'Fine,' he replied, 'and I've checked yours.'

My brain whirled, trying to remember what came next. *Ah, yes:* 'Direct feed is connected and in place.'

'Fine.'

'And your air supply is switched on.'

'Yes, and yours is switched on.'

'Basic equipment to the ready!'

'Good – mask, fins and snorkel,' Reg said, checking me. 'Today, we're going to start with adjusting buoyancy. You do this by inflating and deflating your life jacket. The

Some species also defend themselves against their enemies by swimming in vast shoals. This has the effect of confusing any predator, since it must first isolate a given fish before attacking.

The world of the coral reef is quite a violent one, with fish that are weak or injured falling prey to others that are stronger or more ferocious. This ferocity is very much a characteristic of their acute instinct for survival – in

Day 3 continued

air for this travels to your jacket via the direct feed hose, attached at one end to the first stage of the demand valve, and at the other to this tube here—' He held up the large corrugated tube leading from his life jacket.

'The controls for inflation and deflation are here at the end. You play these two buttons like the bagpipes – this one on the side to go up, and this one on the top, holding it above you, to go down.'

'OK,' I said, mimicking him as he pushed the two buttons at the top end of the tube.

fact, reef fish can display a degree of courage that would be considered ridiculously extreme by human standards. And even more than defending their own lives, these fish will guard their eggs with single-minded determination: the survival of the species takes precedence over all else.

If spitting into your mask isn't your style, you could try moistening the inside of the face plate with half a raw potato or a piece of bladder wrack (a kind of seaweed). Alternatively, you can buy a tube of special liquid to prevent misting up.

GUL

Day 3 continued

Reg seemed satisfied that I was ready. 'Now we're going to do some exercises. To start, we'll kneel on the bottom and then do some controlled-buoyancy ascents and descents, very slowly to the top and back again. I'll show you how first. The second exercise is swimming through the mid-water, adjusting your buoyancy so that you're always in the middle.' He looked at me sternly, but with a twinkle in his eye. 'You'll lose brownie points if I find you at the top or at the bottom. OK?'

'OK,' I replied, thinking longingly of a mug of steaming black coffee.

'Now, mask on . . . mouthpiece . . . Any problems?'

'Uh uh,' I mumbled through the rubber, but I did remember to give the appropriate hand signal for us to go down. Somehow that 'thumbs down' seemed a bit ominous.

I needn't have worried. Once we got below the surface and began to swim, hand in hand, to a deeper level for the buoyancy exercises. I lost all my fear. The water was crystal clear, and shoals of fish were swimming in and out of huge lumps

Coral

The stony coral that we've all come to associate with tropical seas is, in fact, very much alive. Masses of tiny animals known as *polyps* group together to form a colony, and then excrete calcium carbonate (i.e. limestone) to form the outer skeletons – called *exoskeletons* – that we know as coral. You can see where each polyp is located by the openings in the mass: each one is a 'mouth', surrounded by tentacles that grab prey and carry it into the polyp's gullet.

When many colonies of coral occur together, reefs are formed. There are three types of these: *fringing reefs* that lie a short distance from the shore; *barrier reefs* (like the Great Barrier Reef off Australia) that lie a greater distance from the shore and are separated from it by a deep channel; and *atolls* that are ring-shaped

Day 3 continued

Despite their popular image, some types of coral don't produce stony outer skeletons. These 'soft corals' tend to form huge congregations of individual polyps, and are famous for the variety and beauty of their colours, all shades of blue, pink, orange and green. Their other remarkable characteristic is that they swell at night, resuming their normal size during the day. One variety was observed to reach a height of over 40 centimetres, almost six times its daytime size.

of coral. Fish of all shapes, sizes and, most of all, colours – brown, black, yellow, blue, red, golden and mixtures of all these. One coral outcrop caught my eye: *hundreds* of orange anthias were congregating there. It was extraordinary – they were just like hordes of goldfish!

Nothing down here was like *anything* on the surface – there was so much to see that I felt like Alice in Wonderland. In these shallow waters, the sunlight trickling down from above played amazing tricks with all the colours of the coral and fish, making everything luminous, iridescent and enchanting. The coral itself was not always what it seemed: clumps of soft-looking fronds that seemed to be swaying in the current turned out to be quite stiff, while other, more solid hunks were as soft and floppy as old balloons. It was difficult to tear myself away from all this to follow Reg's instructions, but then it was back to the game of follow my leader . . .

We obviously could no longer talk, but nevertheless, Reg kept checking to make sure that I was all right. An 'OK?' hand signal (thumb and forefinger making an 'O') from him always elicited an 'OK' signal from me – I was feeling fine.

We floated to a stop at a depth of about 4 metres. Gesturing to the direct feed leading from his life jacket, Reg signalled that he was going to make a controlled ascent

and surround a lagoon.

Coral polyps can live no deeper than, at the very most, 90 metres because of their dependence on a certain type of algae that live in their tissues. Acting as a diet supplement as well as a waste remover, the algae cannot survive without sunlight. But what about the coral that can be found up to 1600 metres below the surface? One theory is that the coral began to develop at the optimum depth – say,

Day 3 continued

and descent. Pushing the button on the side of the tube, he gently rose in the water. Then pushing the button on the top and holding the end of the tube over his head, he slowly descended to float beside me. It was an impressive display.

He signalled that it was now my turn. At first, it had seemed silly, needing a life jacket when you were going to be swimming underwater. However, I now began to see its importance, both in helping me to avoid grovelling about on the bottom as I lost the buoyancy in my wet suit with depth, and to save my life if the need arose.

I hesitantly pushed the inflation button and gradually rose to the surface. Then I held the tube above my head and pressed the other button. Down I sank, landing with a thud beside Reg.

Reg made me go up and down innumerable times until I got the hang of it. Finally, I was able to ascend slowly and majestically

in the shallows of a volcanic island – and when the sea level rose as the volcano sank, the coral kept pace with this gradual change, leaving behind exo-skeletons as it grew to a great height.

However, coral demands certain conditions before it will grow at all. The water must be warm – no colder than about 20°C (68°F). It must also be free of pollution and sediment (that's why there's no coral off the coasts of Brazil, West Africa and eastern India, where great rivers empty), and there must be a good current, to bring food and oxygen and to carry off waste.

Increasing pollution of the earth's oceans has done much to destroy coral reefs, as has the use of explosives for fishing and the predation by parrotfish and certain types of starfish, all of which eat coral. However, that said, a huge area of our

Day 3 continued

towards the surface like the best of them. My descent was accomplished with the same aplomb, and Reg, sharing my pleasure, showed his approval by silently clapping.

Now it was time to see if I could swim through the water adjusting my buoyancy as I went along. First, Reg swam effortlessly around me, pushing the buttons on his direct feed tube every now and then to alter his depth. I noticed that he inflated and deflated his life jacket only in very short bursts, and I tried to imitate him when my turn came. The further I swam, the easier it became to judge how much adjustment I needed, and soon I was swimming quite competently, moving forward by finning, my left hand occupied with the buttons.

Once I had got the technicalities off pat, I was able simply to enjoy the sensation of being underwater. Now I could dangle in mid-water like Peter Pan caught in mid-swoop, and I began to relax as I discovered that I didn't have to make any movement at all with my hands or fins – just a subtle adjustment to the air in my jacket and I could hover on the spot. It gave me a real kick, this freedom of movement that, before, had seemed to belong to a different species of life.

I've always been mesmerized by the way fish move – quivering near something that interests them and then, with just a twitch of their fins, darting off. Now I could give a good imitation of them. Everything seemed to be in slow motion, and I moved along with the grace and dreaminess of an astronaut. It really was the most sensuous feeling.

I took my time to look about me

In tropical waters, don't touch or play with any fish that appear passive or unconcerned. This usually means that they have an effective (and unpleasant) defence mechanism – a sting or poisonous spines.

planet is still covered by coral – about 80 million square miles, or 25 times the area of Europe – much of which has endured for 200 million years and parts of which are, today, alive and ever-changing.

There are about 2500 different types of coral, varying in shape and colour – white, pink, blue, purple, red, yellow, golden brown, black. One of the most widespread is staghorn coral, with branches resembling a deer's antlers. Red coral, often seen in jewellery, is found in the Mediterranean, and generally develops separately from reefs. Black coral is extremely hard, and is much prized by Arabs, who fashion it into beads and necklaces.

Day 3 continued

and feast my eyes on this submerged world. It was like swimming in a huge aquarium. One fish was distinctive: brown and cream, large and ugly. It was hard to miss as it swam over the sandy sea floor, but as it neared a coral outcrop, it virtually disappeared, so effective was its camouflage. I later learned it was a stonefish, an extremely poisonous and dangerous animal. And I'd been swimming close to it!

There are almost 5000 species of sponges – red, yellow, blue; fan-, sphere- and finger-shaped; 1 centimetre to 2 metres tall – but despite this almost infinite variety, they are the simplest of multi-cellular animals. On their own, they reproduce by budding or sending out spores, but they are also 'farmed': a living sponge is cut up, and once the pieces have attached themselves to something solid, new individuals will grow.

Day 3 continued

Reg signalled for me to follow him back to the shore. After the serenity and beauty of the underwater world, the sight of that lovely beach surrounded by barbed wire was distinctly strange, as was the gun-toting soldier gawping at us as we emerged.

'That was great!' I enthused, removing my mask. 'That coral!'

'I'm glad you liked it – the exercises went very well, too.'

'It's fantastic being in the sea.' I was dying to go back down.

'Well, wait till you see Sharm-el-Sheikh – we're going there tomorrow, and we'll be diving off the *Lady Jenny*. That's the diving boat we're booked on.'

'Bit different, eh?'

'It'll be superb. You wait and see.'

It can be revealed that Reg, the fish and I hadn't been alone down there. It would be lovely to say that we'd been floating in a deserted underwater paradise – well, we had been . . . apart from 10 metres of trailing cable, a mad director/camerman and Ray, the stills photographer, who managed to wander into every shot!

First, we'd been filmed near the shore while Reg was briefing me on adjusting buoyancy. The light *was* beautiful at that time of the morning, but the film crew found that it was too early to cope with deep water and trousers, as they waded up to their thighs filming Reg and me disappearing into the sea.

Once we got underwater, the difficulties of this type of filming became really apparent. (The shots at the hotel pool had been infinitely simpler to do.) When you're on land, you just take for granted the instructions you're given, but now, we had somehow to add to Reg's international signals, to come up with a communication system that would be relevant to the job at hand. For example, how do you mime 'Do that once more, but swim out of shot

Surface marker buoys and flags

Currents, tides and natural curiosity can all cause divers to find themselves a long way away from their cover boat when they surface. To make sure that those on board can follow their divers' progress across the seabed and move the boat accordingly, the dive leader will carry down a line from a surface market buoy, or SMB.

An SMB is usually a float that is weighted on the bottom so that it doesn't turn turtle; there are also, however, round ones that are inflated by mouth. A mast can be attached to the top side which carries a blue and white 'A' flag. This is an International Code of Signals flag that, as well as

Day 3 continued

indicating a diver's position, also means: 'There is a diver down; keep clear and proceed at slow speed.' The dive boat itself should also show this signal.

A light line is attached to the underside of the SMB, beneath the surface. This is wound round a reel, which is carried by the dive leader. As the divers descend, he or she unwinds the line, keeping it taut, until the bottom is reached; the line is then locked in place. As the dive continues, the dive leader carries the reel, and the line attached to it pulls the SMB along the surface, marking the divers' position. If necessary, those on the boat can pull on the line to warn the divers to come up. When the dive is finished, the dive leader will rewind the line as he or she ascends.

Day 3 continued

at the end' or 'This time, look that way and do this . . .'? That first day in the sea, everything took an inordinately long time while we tried to understand each other, and until Mike was satisfied.

We were lucky to have Mike Portelly as our director, although I may not have thought so at the time (joke, Mike!). He's had an enormous amount of experience filming underwater – in fact, he's one of the best and very inspiring to work with. But nobody had told me that he is also a lunatic, utterly determined to get the shots he wants, no matter how long it takes. Poor Reg and I were like two naughty schoolchildren being bossed around.

We were, in a funny sort of way, *powerless* underwater with Mike around. We had to do what he told us – we couldn't pipe back and say, 'Hang on a second!' No, we had to sign meekly, 'Yes sir, no sir,' and do what he wanted. I don't think Reg had ever come across anything like this. Here was one of the most respected diving instructors in the world and this mad director was abusing him! It was fortunate that they were already good friends, sharing a love of the sport.

Mike wanted to film Reg and me from every angle, so we had to swim, ascend and descend what seemed like hundreds of times. When Reg was being filmed, I'd sometimes lend a hand, holding a light on him, and he'd do the same when my turn came – no lines of demarcation underwater! Occasionally, Mike would mime tearing out his hair as yet another of the multiplicity of cables littering the seabed got into the shot.

At one point, Mike wanted to film my instructor demonstrating how to adjust buoyancy. Reg shot up towards the surface, far above Mike, and then floated down majestically, right on top of a sharp point of coral – tastefully lit by Graham! One look at the expression on Reg's face and that was it for me – I collapsed into hysterics. It was a very funny feeling, laughing into a mouthpiece, and my hoots of laughter, echoing in my ears, were deafening.

Mike, simultaneously irritated and amused, called a halt while I rolled about helplessly. Eventually, my hysterics became infectious, and I will never forget the sight of all of us on the seabed, holding our sides and shaking with laughter, while Reg looked on bemused.

Finally, after a very long morning, we were allowed to get out of the water, shuffling backwards up to the beach so that we wouldn't trip over our fins. It wasn't even 9.00 a.m., but Graham and Ray's half-hearted enquiries about breakfast were brushed aside by the ever-ebullient Mike, who cried, 'Great! Let's go out in the boat now and get some more shots!'

Hours later, I finally got back to the hotel and into some dry clothes. I felt wonderfully tired, and knew

Day 3 continued

that I'd done a good day's hard work. I also felt extremely fit and healthy – and extremely thin (we still hadn't eaten!).

At long last, I headed back to my room to do my packing in preparation for the trip down the Sinai peninsula the following day. However, even though it was late and the lights of Eilat were like diamonds in the darkness, Mike hadn't finished yet. Oh no, he'd had another great idea: what about a scene with Anneka in bed reading a book about Red Sea fish? (This was something I *had* planned on doing anyway – in privacy!) Soon my room was crowded with equipment and crew, the cameras were set up and I lay in bed, waiting for instructions.

Someone had had the bright idea of ordering some drinks from room service. Just as we were starting to film, there was a knock on the door. The waiter entered, to be greeted by the sight of me lying, seemingly naked, in bed, surrounded by members of the crew in various states of undress (it was very hot under the lights) and Mike leaping on and off my bed saying, 'No, no, no, pretend that you're a bit more asleep' or 'Open your eyes a bit.'

The waiter's eyes almost popped out of his head – the King Solomon's Palace Hotel was obviously playing host to a pornographic video session!

Finally alone, I prepared for bed (for real this time), my room and reputation in tatters. Would we ever dare to come back?

Mike with his underwater camera

DAY 4

Stars, feathers, cucumbers and urchins

Some of the most intriguing creatures you may meet on the sea floor are the echinoderms, which include starfish, feather stars, sea cucumbers and sea urchins.

All echinoderms owe at least some of their beauty to their symmetry – all of them consist of five parts around a central axis. However, while this is obvious in, say, the five-legged starfish, it's only when you dissect it that the submarine-shaped sea cucumber (given this name by the Roman naturalist Pliny the Elder almost 2000 years ago) reveals a similar structure. And even multi-legged starfish – for example, the sunstar, which has 10 or more legs – are actually composed of five basic

Day 4 continued

Shortly after dawn, we finally got everything packed away into and on top of our little minibus, and drove the short distance to the Taba Beach checkpoint on the Egyptian border. Considering that the Israelis and Egyptians were at war only a comparatively short time ago, the checkpoint was surprisingly sleepy and ramshackle: an old gate, a bit of barbed wire and a couple of chairs.

It was all hands on deck as we transferred our tons of carefully stowed equipment and other luggage out of the minibus and into antiquated supermarket trolleys provided by Israeli customs. Then, after a few formalities, we had to take all our things out of the Israeli trolleys and into some Eygptian ones, and push these through no-man's-land to the Egyptian side. This was too much like hard work . . .

Timelessness was definitely the order of the day here; no one was going anywhere in a hurry. The few soldiers who peered out of the huts and spartan offices long enough to swot the flies away and nod to us, as we trundled, cursing, yet another trolley through, were the sole reminders of the long-standing feud with the Israelis. It was like a scene from *Gunfight at the OK Corral* – except that their eyes were not squinting in hatred, but against the dazzling sun.

There were so many forms to fill in that we suspected that the Egyptians must have had a hot line to the Foreign Office. There were even forms to fill in in order to fill in other forms! And while I'm not absolutely sure, I don't think I saw any filing cabinets in the customs office – there *was* an enormous bonfire out back, however . . .

The customs officials, nodding and grinning encouragingly, were very friendly as they kept us waiting. Maybe we were the most interesting bunch they'd had

parts radiating from a central axis.

All the echinoderms possess a complex internal system of fluid-filled canals that extend outside their bodies to form tube feet. These are responsible for respiration, feeding and, in many species, movement: the contraction of muscles and the movement of water in and out raise and lower the feet. The sea urchin's feet end in suckers that can be extended beyond its poisonous spines if the creature wants to climb a vertical rock.

The echinoderms vary in their method of feeding and their chosen food. Sea urchins shuffle over rocks, their elaborate mouths – comprising 20 different parts and located right in the centre of the lower surface – rasping off tiny plants and animals. Starfish, on the other hand, make do

Day 4 continued

through for a few days. We certainly must have made quite a spectacle with our 60 – yes, *60* – items of luggage and equipment.

They make friends easily, these Egyptians. I seemed to go down particularly well with the chief customs officer, who tried to find out from Mike how much he could buy me for. I just kept nodding and smiling as I walked slowly backwards towards the minibus on the other side of the barrier. When I got close enough, I gave a little wave – *byeee* – and ran for it!

We were so glad to get through in apparently record time – only two hours – that we dug into our *Lady Jenny* survival kit. There's a time and a place for champagne, and this wasn't really either, but it seemed such a good idea . . .

The most surprising thing about driving through the Sinai was that it wasn't anything like I thought a desert should be: flat as far as the eye could see, full of mirages of Coca-Cola stands and blue lagoons. I was definitely in the wrong film. The strip of dead straight road did shimmer in the heat (by now, the temperature was soaring into the 100s), but on either side were the most magnificent bare, rocky mountains, and each gap through them revealed valleys with even more mountain ranges beyond.

There was no living creature for miles. Occasionally, however, we were delighted by a straggle of haughty camels and, in the distance, away from the main road, huddles of small, brightly coloured

with shellfish, prising open bivalves such as oysters and clams with their suckered arms; they then invert the stomach and place it on their victim, which is dissolved by the digestive juices and then sucked up.

Others are less violent: the sedentary feather star relies on organic particles that float to it; the sea cucumber extracts nutrients from the sand and mud it draws in through its ten tentacles. One echinoderm – the crown-of-thorns starfish – lives on the polyps that create coral and, as a result, has greatly damaged some of the reefs of the Pacific Ocean.

All of these animals have developed extremely effective methods of protection. As many swimmers and divers are only too aware, sea urchins have needle-sharp spines, which in some species are also poisonous; in

Day 4 continued

tents that must have been bedouin settlements.

Just when the journey was beginning to pall – some 3 hours later – there was a sight for (literally) sore eyes: not a mirage, nor a figment of our poor, dusty imaginations, but real, blue, salty, wavy, glistening, inviting, cool sea. As we turned to drive along the coast, there was a crop of road signs, bearing what looked like hieroglyphics. We strained to extract something intelligible from them, and finally made out exactly what we'd wanted to see: SHARM-EL-SHEIKH. As far as we knew, it might also have said 'Not this way' or '100 miles to . . .', but our high spirits were rewarded by the minibus swinging into the tiny port just a few minutes later.

We arrived about noon, and as we approached the port, our hearts sank as we saw that we'd entered yet another military zone – Sharm-el-Sheikh is an Egyptian naval base

addition, they also have small pincers on their tough outer covering, some of which contain poison and are used for defence. Sea cucumbers can shoot out sticky white threads to protect themselves; they also have the strange habit of expelling some of their internal organs when they're frightened. Whether this is a form of peace offering to attackers is unknown, but they are able to regenerate a new set of organs within six weeks.

This extraordinary ability to regenerate – like so many marine Doctor Who's – is found in other echinoderms. Starfish, in particular, are extremely good at it, being able to grow back arms at will, and broken pieces of some species are able to form into completely new individuals!

Day 4 continued

and the security there was as hot as the weather. We were stopped at a customs post and the whole bureaucratic procedure began again. This time, as well as all the palaver of checking our equipment, luggage and passports, we were held up for ages while the only official who could sign the papers to let us on the boat disappeared to have his lunch!

When we at last reached the pier, I'd had about as much red tape as I could stomach. However, the sight of the *Lady Jenny*, and the greeting we received from the skipper Adrian and from Alex and Tamara, the boat's divemasters, cheered me up considerably. For the last time (for a while at least), we unloaded the minibus and passed across our luggage and equipment, and then climbed awkwardly over the side of the boat and on to the deck ourselves.

Everyone on board the *Lady Jenny* looked as if they'd stepped from the pages of a health magazine – fit, bronzed, smiling. As well as Adrian, Alex and Tamara, the crew consisted of an out-of-work actor who had come along as cook for the fun of it; three super girls (two from New Zealand) who worked in the kitchen; an engineer; and a few extra helpers – and all of them were experienced divers. The boat was a lovely, large, old wooden dame with old brass lanterns and worn panelling. It could accommodate about 20 guests, among them now a group of six French diving doctors.

Tamara showed me to my cabin.

Seafans (or gorgonians) are actually related to jellyfish, but unlike their cousins, they congregate in vast colonies and secrete calcium to form a flexible skeleton; in this way, they are very similar to coral. The skeletal fans are attached firmly to the seabed or to rocks, and can be any one of a dozen colours, from purple to brilliant red, yellow and orange.

They are found in oceans all over the world, but in tropical seas they can achieve relatively great heights, up to 1.2–1.5 metres. There are few things more breath-taking than a 'forest' of seafans, waving gently in the current.

Day 4 continued

It was tiny, with one porthole, but later I found out how lucky I was to be in such splendid isolation: the male members of the film crew had to sleep four to a cabin. No wonder Ray finally gave up and slept on deck under the stars!

Almost as soon as we boarded the boat, Adrian gave orders for us to get underway for the voyage further down the coast to a place called The Alternatives, an offshore coral reef. After the long drive and the tedium of Egyptian bureaucracy, the moment the *Lady Jenny* moved away from the dock, trailing a Zodiac (a solid-hull inflatable) in her wake, we all felt as if we'd left civilization – and all its paperwork – behind.

Of course, our steaming out of port wasn't as simple as that – not when you're filming all this for posterity. First, we had to sail a little way out of the port while Graham, back on the dock, filmed us leaving. Then we had to go back, pick him up and wait while he set up to film

Sharm-el-Sheikh fading into the distance from the boat. And on TV it looks so easy!

During the two-hour sail, Tamara

In 1982, in the Mediterranean off Cavalaire, just south of St Tropez, Patrick Raude and five other divers left and returned to their diving bell *Petrel* when it was at a depth of 501 metres.

Day 4 continued

pulled out a map and showed us where we would be diving for the next few days, and we relaxed for a bit while we discussed our plans.

'Why is it called "The Alternatives"?' I asked. Adrian, joining us from the bridge for a moment, said with a smirk that it was because it's always a good alternative – ask a silly question! Reg, who had dived this area a great deal, and quite often from the *Lady Jenny*, told me that The Alternatives, being nice and shallow (a maximum of 10 metres), would be the ideal place to

Day 4 continued

continue my training, and especially excellent for my first serious dive from a boat.

As we neared our destination, we got into our swimsuits, dug out all our gear and, bringing it up on deck, checked it thoroughly.

'It's quite daunting suddenly being on a boat, Reg. Is it going to be very different?'

'You'll find it so easy, Annie,' he replied. 'There's plenty of room to change, a ladder, everything. You're going to love it. It's much easier than going in from the beach.'

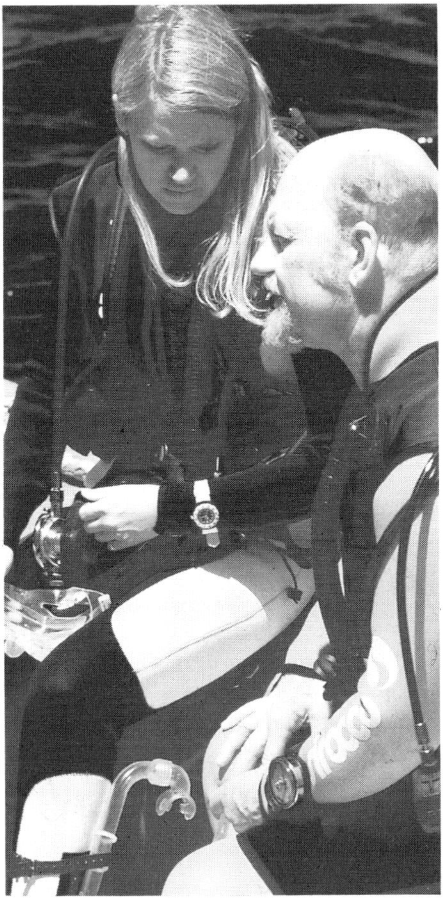

'What *is* daunting is just hopping into the sea. You don't know *anything* about what's round you.' I was really looking for reassurance now.

'Well, this is where it's all going to happen, and you'll love every moment.'

Reg wasn't being any help at all!

At that moment, we felt the boat's engine stop, and all my worries had to retreat to the back of my mind while I got into my wet suit, donned my 'stab' jacket, pulled on my cylinder and began the pre-dive check with Reg.

When we'd finished and were sure that neither of us had forgotten to make a vital connection or had left an important piece of equipment behind in our cabins, Reg held up his hand.

'You're going down deeper than you've been before,' he said. 'You must remember to take it easy on the way down. On the way back *up*, don't forget that you should only ascend as fast as the small bubbles. And never hold your breath as you come up.

'Because you're going to be diving deeper than before, I want you to wear this waterproof watch and this depth gauge today. I'll be keeping track of how deep we go and for how long, but I want you to be aware, too. This is something you'll have to know when it comes to reading a decompression table. I'll explain more about that tonight.'

Day 4 continued

Reg continued: 'Today we're going to do some mask clearing, including taking off the mask completely – don't look so worried, Anneka! – and sharing air in this deeper water. Ready?'

This time we were going to jump into the sea from the side of the *Lady Jenny*. Reg told me to hold on to my mask with one hand and press my contents gauge against my side with the other. Manoeuvring with difficulty because of my fins, I finally took up my position on the side and peered down: the drop was a good deal further than the side of the pool. I braced myself for a second, but after watching everyone else

Depth gauges and timing devices

Because it is vital to know how deep you are diving, you will need a depth gauge. Your instructor should watch this for you during your initial dives.

Depth gauges are sometimes calibrated up to 80 metres, even though sport divers are not advised to go any deeper than 50 metres. (If metric is a mystery to you, you can also get ones calibrated in feet.) They have to be very accurate if they are to be of any use. To ensure this, you can have them pressure tested – say, at a dive shop. The gauge is put in a small tank of water that is then compressed by degrees; the reading on the gauge is checked at 10-metre intervals to make sure that it matches the known pressure in the tank.

Some gauges have a 'maximum

Day 4 continued

plop in happily and barely sink below the surface, I took a deep breath and let it happen.

After giving Reg a big OK sign to show him that I was quite happy, we started to nose-dive down. He seemed to descend very smoothly, but that first time, I had to struggle a little inelegantly to catch up. Although this was partly because I hadn't got my weights quite right, mostly it could be chalked up to inexperience – by the end of the week, I was floating down effortlessly.

Here the seabed was 10 metres down, and with a tremendous feeling of freedom and weightlessness, I cavorted to my heart's content. Somersaulting in slow motion and weaving in and out of some very deep clefts in the reef, I felt like a child on the first day of a school holiday.

The coral was extremely beautiful, even more so than at Taba Beach, and there seemed to be an

depth' needle that records the deepest level to which you have dived; this, I was told, helps when it comes to calculating decompression times. Some glow in the dark, another useful feature.

Some sort of timing device is another essential, again for decompression calculations. Water- and pressure-proof diving watches can range from the most basic to analogue watches resistant to pressures at 150 metres. All diving watches have a movable outer rim (called a 'bezel') that is set when you leave the surface; the minute hand will then show exactly how long you've been down.

Alternatively, you can use a dive timer. This starts up automatically as you begin your descent, and an alarm can be set so that it will sound when the scheduled duration of the dive has been reached.

Day 4 continued

infinite variety – solid stubby fingers, delicate, skinny branches, great chunks arranged in swirls. Darting in and out of the openings were thousands of fish, a play of light and shadow as the schools passed us. Sea anemones waved sensuously in the current, yellow-and-white clownfish peeking out from among the fronds . . . It was strange that the barren wastelands of the Sinai should end here in the rich walls of coral of the Red Sea. It was all breathtaking. No longer did I have to fantasize – this really was *The Undersea World of Anneka Rice*!

Reg called a halt and signalled for me to watch him. First, he took off his mask (his face suddenly looking very bare) and placed it on the seabed; then he retrieved it, put it back on and cleared it by pressing on its top edge and breathing out. Then it was my turn.

The sand on the bottom had been stirred up, and as I removed the mask, placed it on the seabed and

opened my now-unprotected eyes, the visibility was pretty poor, making me doubt for a moment whether I'd be able to find it again. The water was very salty, too, and my eyes began to sting. But then I put my hand out, found my mask, put it on and, for once, cleared it with no trouble.

I was quite proud of my achievement, but this feeling rapidly wore off as I had to repeat my triumph endlessly for the camera. (If nothing else, repeated 'takes' ensure that you do an awful lot of practice!)

A fish among the tentacles

Although marine life under the ocean waves seems to reflect a 'kill or be killed' philosophy, there are a number of examples of extraordinary co-operation. One such involves the relationship between sea anemones and clownfish.

Anemones are solitary animals that cling to rocks or shells. Lacking a skeleton, their bodies consist of a cylinder of muscle topped by hollow tentacles. The latter wave about in the current, inviting tiny marine organisms, small fishes and crabs to venture into their soft embrace.

Once there, however, stinging cells (*nematoblasts*) in the tentacles deliver paralysing venom to the prey, and

Day 4 continued

the barbed ends draw the struggling animal into the depths of the fronds to the digestive cavity within. However, as deadly as it may seem to one of its victims, if an anemone is disturbed, its tentacles withdraw into the cavity in a flash so that it resembles a fleshy stump.

There is, however, one animal that's unaffected by either the anemone's stings or its transformation into a muscular cylinder: the clownfish (also known as the clown anemonefish). It is well named: with its orangy-yellow body, set off by white bands at its neck, middle and tail, it looks as if it's ready for the circus ring. While other fish in the coral reef dart hither and thither in search of a safe harbour, the clownfish finds one within the tentacles of the sea anemone.

Day 4 continued

There was also a strong current, and just trying to stay in one place while I knelt took all my strength. However, I reckon that, now, if I ever lose my mask anywhere for any reason. I'll have no trouble being able to cope.

Then Reg signalled again, this time the 'karate chop' to the neck that indicated that he had lost his air supply. I took a breath, then placed my mouthpiece in his mouth for him to take two breaths, then back to me for two more and so on until Reg was satisfied that I knew what I was doing.

At this depth, my cylinder lasted about an hour, but it was only when the arrow on my contents gauge pointed to the danger area that Mike let me go back up.

As I ascended, I kept an eye on the small bubbles I was exhaling, making sure that I didn't go any faster than they did. It was fascinating to watch some of the larger bubbles and see how they swelled as they neared the surface. No wonder you had to breathe out quite a lot as you go up – just imagine what those bubbles could do to your lungs!

'That was unbelievable!' I ex-

For some reason, as yet not understood, the clownfish is immune to the anemone's venom, which is fatal to other fish. It cleans and feeds the anemone and stimulates its tentacles, while the anemone, in turn, shelters the clownfish and protects it against dangers in the sea outside. The fish even mates within the fronds, and its eggs are laid next to the anemone, which will give them the same sort of protection.

A clownfish will not usually leave its home among the tentacles except to get food for its host. However, it will fight with other fish to do this, and divers have found that, if they come within a metre or so of an anemone, these tiny fish will often attack them by pecking at their masks.

Day 4 continued

claimed as Reg and I reached the *Jenny*'s ladder. 'But I have half a ton of the Sinai peninsula in my eye.' I rubbed it, still suffering from the mask clearing. 'That was the best dive yet. Quite incredible what's down there. Those tiny silver fishes – they were like pins of light, then you get near and saw they were actually fishes. That was brilliant, Reg. Ready for coffee?'

We mounted the ladder and were met by Tamara, logbook at the ready.

'It was fantastic, wonderful,' I burbled, still full of enthusiasm for what I'd seen.

'OK, Anneka,' she said effici-

The biggest hazards to surfacing divers are approaching boats that haven't seen them. When surfacing in water with good visiblity, look up to scan the surface for boats. If the visibility is poor, surface with a hand raised above your head so that the hand will hit any obstacle before your head!

The Red Sea is living evidence of catastrophic changes in the earth's surface. It is, in fact, a giant rift in its crust, separating Africa from Asia, a cleft that was formed by the spreading of the sea floor.

Day 4 continued

ently, 'how about giving me your dive details, starting with bottom time?'

'I have no idea.' I looked over to Reg for help. I'd completely forgotten to check.

He gave it: 'Bottom time 35 minutes, 40 minutes duration, 10 metres.'

'That's exactly what I said without moving my lips!'

That day, we were down for a total of nearly three hours, with only two ten-minute breaks in between. The shoot took longer than expected because, for some reason, our communication system didn't work so well this time – Mike stamped his fin in exasperation as we tried to follow his underwater instructions . . . badly. If I hadn't been doing it for filming, we could have completed this part of my training in a 30-minute dive. However, despite being terribly tired, I also felt exhilarated when we'd finished because I knew that

we'd got the shots in the end. And I did have the memory of Alex, off camera, chasing fish into shot . . .

I *was* relieved to get back on the boat, although it was quite a hassle trying to wash the salt out of my hair, and to get dry and dressed in the tiny communal shower room. After several attempts at making myself presentable, I simply gave up, preferring the wild 'mermaid look' and living in flip-flops and shorts until we got back to civilization.

I was looking forward to dinner, and I made my way to the dining

No one knows the true origin of the term 'the bends'. Some say that it came about because afflicted divers were paralysed into such odd shapes; others claim that it was because the position in which divers became paralysed resembled a fashion known as the 'Grecian bend'.

Decompression sickness is also called 'caisson disease': caissons are pressurized chambers or diving bells with open bottoms, which are used underwater to lay foundations for construction work.

The *re*compression chamber used in the treatment of decom-

Day 4 continued

area just off the central galley. How they produced so many wonderful meals in such a tiny kitchen was a source of constant amazement. They dished up a kind of exotic school food – really lovely curries and terrific puddings – and meals were announced with a *'Come and get it!'* by the 'Singing Cook' (the

A working supper

out-of-work actor), who accompanied his vocals by bashing two pan lids together.

There was also lots to eat, which was just as well since we all shovelled in as much as we could when Mike would let us. 'Lunch? What's that?' he would say when one of us, stricken with hunger pangs, dared to broach the subject. He got so absorbed in his work that, if we hadn't reminded him, we would never have eaten. As it was, all we could usually manage before being called back to work was just a sandwich, but because he was so enthusiastic, it seemed churlish to complain. Still, by the end of filming I'd lost at least half a stone, from the sheer amount of diving I'd done and because I was kept so busy and rarely had time to eat.

After dinner, Reg and I repaired to the deck to watch the sun go down, a lovely sight that went some way towards modifying the horrors of his decompression lecture. There we were, moored miles away from any town, just a stark landscape, no settlements, no houses, nothing as far as the eye could see. It was very beautiful and very peaceful – I don't

pression sickness is sometimes confused with the *de*compression chamber used by commercial divers undertaking work at deep depths. The latter, however, is very different. After divers enter a decompression chamber on the surface (or part of the way down), the air inside (usually a mixture of gases) is compressed to that found at the depth where they'll be working; the chamber (containing the divers) is then lowered to the desired depth. When the work is finished and they're finally back on the surface, the divers undergo gradual decompression – that is, the air in the chamber will be allowed to leak out slowly, thus becoming less compressed (i.e. the opposite of recompression).

Day 4 continued

think I've ever felt so remote from the rest of the world.

While Reg and I talked, the others abandoned their tiny cabins and joined us on deck, drinking beer, playing cards, talking over what they'd done during the day. Our lot didn't stop working; when we weren't actually filming, cameras would be checked and loaded, and the engineering side of the shoot would be sorted out.

There was, however, another reason why the other guests came up on deck instead of relaxing in their cabins: when we were filming on board, the boat's generator had to be turned off, which meant that there wasn't any air conditioning and no one could even go to the loo. Considering that they hadn't known that they'd be taking part in a video when they'd booked their holiday, they were a long-suffering but terrific bunch.

After he'd finished his lecture, Reg surprised me with 'How would you feel about a night dive?'

'You must be joking!' I exclaimed, caught off guard. 'Any diving I'm going to do tonight is straight into bed.'

Then I noticed that the French divers, who had gone below deck a few minutes before, had reappeared all kitted up. As they descended the ladder to the Zodiac floating in the darkness surrounding the boat, they looked as if they were all going on some desperately secret mission.

While they were away, we sat in the lounge and Mike showed us videos of some of the underwater feature films he'd done. It was extraordinary, watching those videos, listening to the comments of the experienced divers around me and knowing that tomorrow we were going to see more of one of the best diving areas in the world.

They all seemed to know each other – 'Oh, Mark, he used to dive off the Barrier Reef with Fred, you know . . .' – and I realized that

The nitrogen frothing in the blood during decompression sickness resembles the bubbling of carbon dioxide in a bottle of champagne when it's uncorked!

In 1978, at the height of the oil boom, 1500 of the world's professional divers – about one-third of the total – were employed in the North Sea. One company, Shell Mex, was spending $1500 a minute on their diving operation.

Day 4 continued

Decompression

I was of two minds about this lecture from Reg. I was dreading hearing about more of the horrible things that can happen to you when you're diving, but equally, I had a kind of morbid fascination to know all of the grim details.

When you breathe compressed air at depth, although it feels as if you're breathing normally, you are actually inhaling more and more air each time – the air being thicker to compensate for the water pressure. Of this air, 79 per cent is nitrogen, a gas that our bodies have no use for. On the surface, it gradually dissolves in the blood and fatty tissues before being excreted and, as such, doesn't do us any harm. But if we stay too deep for too long and then come straight back to the surface, the body can't hold the extra amount of nitrogen in solution. On ascent, as it expands with the reduced pressure, it forms into bubbles in the bloodstream, which can result in *decompression sickness*, a dangerous condition commonly known as 'the bends'.

Most of the people who are stupid enough not to follow the rules and stay down too long do so because they are diving for gain. Just a few minutes more to pick up a few extra crayfish, gold bars, etc. and they put themselves at personal risk.

'A British diver I knew,' said Reg, 'went down and saw enough crayfish to pay off his mortgage and buy a new car. The temptation was too great. He's now dead – not by drowning, but from the bends.

'I used to teach Tunisian sponge divers,' he continued, 'and I drummed the dangers of decompression sickness into them. But they would see enough sponges to buy four camels or ten wives or the like. Six months later, some were dead and many more were paralysed.'

The symptoms and the cure

The symptoms of decompression sickness can be subdivided into two classes.

Class I symptoms occur if you stay down a little too long or if, on a perfectly correct dive, you are simply unlucky – everyone's body reacts differently. The most common symptoms are aches and pains, varying from a gentle throb to an agonizing pain, usually (but not invariably) in the joints that have just been used – in the knees if swimming a lot or the elbows if you've been lifting.

'The trouble with serious divers – "hairy divers" as they're known – is that they're always reluctant to admit that they're in any pain,' said Reg. 'They just shrug off any symptom as slight muscle strain.'

The joint pain can be preceded by a slight itchy rash and/or swellings on the hands – what the helmet divers called 'ants and sheep' because it felt like ants walking over their hands and the swellings reminded them of sheep.

Class II symptoms are a different matter. Like the Class I variety, they include pain in the joints, but this can be accompanied by dizziness,

Day 4 continued

headache, chest pains, shortness of breath, confusion, numbness or paralysis, partial blindness, loss of balance, lack of control. In fact, the helmet divers called them 'the staggers and shakes' because of the way the nitrogen bubbles affect the central nervous system. The paralysis that occurs from the waist down is very frequently permanent.

While the symptoms of burst lung occur within a few minutes, those for decompression sickness can take a lot longer:

- 75% of cases show symptoms within ½ hour of surfacing.
- 85% within 1 hour.
- 95% within 3 hours.

The symptoms of the remaining 5 per cent can take anything up to 24 hours to become apparent.

As with burst lung, the only course of action for decompression sickness is to go (or be taken) as soon as possible to a recompression chamber. Here, when the air pressure surrounding your body is compressed to the same level as the water you have left, the nitrogen bubbles will gradually become smaller until they dissolve in your blood and tissues and are excreted.

Because symptoms can take some time to appear, if you have only skin problems it is still a good idea to find out where the nearest recompression chamber is. (In fact, you should always find this out *before* doing any diving at all.) Then, if joint pain (or any other symptom) begins, make sure you get to it quickly. It will help a lot if you can breathe pure oxygen on the way.

Avoiding the bends; using a table

To prevent decompression sickness, divers today use decompression tables. If they'd been invented 200 years earlier, a lot more people would have lived. Back then, the helmet divers believed that 'When the water is cold and murky, you will suffer from the bends.' Then in 1878, a French scientist called Paul Bert realized that the problem was due to the nitrogen's dissolving in the blood and forming bubbles. Unfortunately, he didn't tell the helmet divers about it.

Luckily, at the turn of the century, the Royal Navy became concerned about why their divers were becoming afflicted by this strange and incapacitating illness, and they called in the Scottish scientist John Scott Haldane. He was familiar with Bert's book *La pression barometrique*, and decided that he could probably work out some rules and formulate a useful table.

When he'd done this, he tested it, using himself and his assistants as guinea pigs in a recompression chamber. For example, he would say, 'Take me down to 90 feet, leave me there for four hours, then bring me up and let's see what happens.' When the nitrogen in his body caused symptoms of 'the bends', he knew that something was wrong!

So by this laborious method of trial and error – which must have been quite painful for Haldane and his men – the first decompression table came to be written, the basis of all the ones in use today.

Day 4 continued

On the *Lady Jenny*, we used the one produced by the Royal Navy Physiological Laboratory for the British Sub-Aqua Club, although there are many other valid tables, produced by the US Navy, the Professional Association of Diving Instructors and others.

stop' dive, and not for 24 hours after one involving decompression stops. If you're diving at altitude a 'depth penalty' may need to be added to the depth as measured on a depth gauge.)

The tables show how long you can remain at a certain depth and still

RNPL/BSAC Air Diving Decompression Table

Descent Rate: 30 metres/minute maximum
Ascent Rate: 15 metres/minute

Maximum Depth (metres)	No Stop Time (minutes)	Bottom Time in Minutes					
10	**232**	431	—	—	—	—	—
12	**137**	140	159	179	201	229	270
14	**96**	98	106	116	125	134	144
16	**72**	73	81	88	94	99	105
18	**57**	59	66	71	76	80	84
20	**46**	49	55	60	63	67	70
Stops at 5 metres (minutes)		**5**	**10**	**15**	**20**	**25**	**30**
22	**38**	42	47	51	55	58	
24	**32**	37	41	45	48	51	
26	**27**	32	37	40	43	45	
28	**23**	29	33	36	39	41	
30	**20**	25	30	33	35	37	
32	**18**	23	27	30	32	34	
34	**16**	21	25	28	30	31	
36	**14**	20	23	26	27	29	
38	**12**	18	21	24	26	27	
40	**11**	17	20	22	24	25	
42	**10**	16	19	21	22	24	
44	**9**	15	18	20	21		
46	**8**	14	17	18	20		
48	**8**	13	16	17			
50	**7**	12	15	17			
Stops at 10 metres / 5 metres (minutes)		**5 / 5**	**5 / 10**	**5 / 15**	**5 / 20**	**5 / 25**	

Not more than 8 hours spent under pressure (submerged) during 24 hours

FOR TWO DIVES ONLY

When Second Dive is less than 9 metres no stop is required

A = Bottom Time in minutes of 1st Dive
B = Bottom Time in minutes of 2nd Dive

Both Dives less than 40 metres

Surface Interval	*Bottom Time*
Up to 2 hours	A + B
2 to 4 hours	$\frac{A}{2}$ + B
4 to 6 hours	$\frac{A}{4}$ + B
More than 6 hours	B

Either Dive more than 40 metres

Surface Interval	*Bottom Time*
Up to 2 hours	A + B
2 to 4 hours	$\frac{A}{2}$ + B
4 to 8 hours	$\frac{A}{4}$ + B
8 to 16 hours	$\frac{A}{8}$ + B
More than 16 hours	B

ALWAYS DECOMPRESS FOR THE **GREATEST** DEPTH REACHED DURING **EITHER** DIVE

('Maximum depth' is the greatest depth reached during a dive, 'no stop time' is the longest 'bottom time' not requiring decompression stops, and bottom time is measured from start of descent to start of ascent. You mustn't fly for 2 hours after a 'non

ascend without stopping – a 'no stop' dive. For example, according to the BSAC/RNPL table, you can spend 46 minutes (including the descent time) at a depth of 20 metres. However, any longer than that and you'll have to make a 'decompression stop', when

Day 4 continued

you simply float in place to give the nitrogen in your body time to dissolve. If you then, say, stay at 20 metres for 3 minutes longer (i.e. a total of 49 minutes), you will have to stop at a depth of 5 metres for 5 minutes.

In addition, you should never descend more quickly than 30 metres per minute (which is really quite fast), and you should never ascend faster than 15 metres per minute. You can tell if you are ascending at the correct speed by going no faster than the small bubbles that escape from your aqualung – not the large ones as these can go too fast.

Beginners should, in fact, make sure that all their early dives do not require decompression stops. You need to have enough air to do these besides the experience in calculating and using the necessary back-up equipment. There should always be a good reason for making any dive that does involve stops. For example, if you're diving to a wreck at 40 metres, you may want to spend more than 11 minutes to photograph it and so on. Even though it is always better to calculate your dive before you leave the boat, you should always carry a decompression table when you dive; some are plastic-covered and can be glued to the sleeve of your diving suit or placed in a pocket.

The only criticism of the BSAC/RNPL table is that it's known to be conservative, particularly in the area of repeat dives – that is, you *may* actually be able to stay down a little longer than the table indicates. However, a diver who says, 'Well, the table says that I can stay for 20 minutes, but I'm sure that 25 will be fine' is beginning to go down a very slippery slope. Divers can appear to get away with the most remarkable things, but when they get unlucky (as they probably will one day), they could be heading for Class II symptoms or worse.

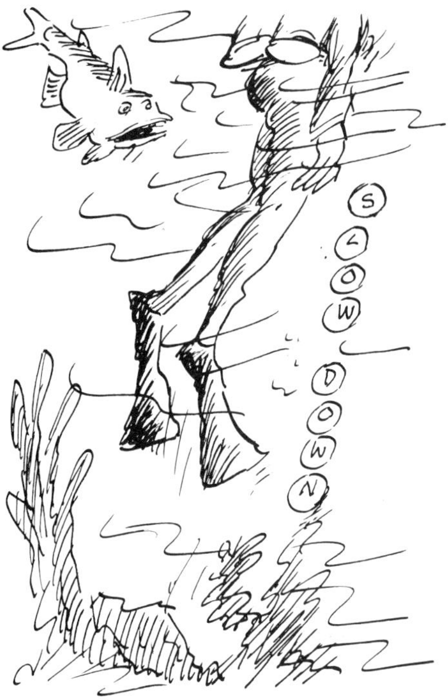

Some good advice:

- If you are going to do repeat dives, always do your deepest one first.
- Always work out on the surface how long you can stay down and what your decompression stops will be. Don't try to calculate this underwater.
- Know how to work out your own times and trust your own tables. Don't be led astray by a cowboy who thinks he can push the limits.

Day 4 continued

relatively few people dive seriously, quite a small, close-knit group. I was later to discover that international diving cuts across all sorts of social boundaries, and attracts an enthusiastic, adventurous type of person. I've since dived with orthopaedic surgeons, museum curators, jewel dealers – all wanting to satisfy an interest or get a new perspective on life. Their closeness undoubtedly springs from the 'buddy mentality': there's nothing that will breed friendship and trust so much as having to depend on someone in a life-or-death situation.

Tonight it was fascinating to lean back, a glass of brandy in hand, listening to everyone's diving tales and finding out what my companions did throughout the year. For example, Alex and Tamara's life simply revolved around diving in the Red Sea; they didn't even have a home in England any more.

As I got ready for bed, I felt more than heard Adrian start up the motor so that we could steam to Ras Muhammed, ready for our morning dive. I went to the porthole and, with the gentle throb of the engine in my ears, looked out. I've been to lots of places where you can see the stars very clearly, but here, down at the bottom of the Sinai, where there's no pollution, no clouds and the air is very dry, you really do feel as though you're looking out from the edge of the planet into nothing – the stars are just so bright.

With a sigh, I got into bed. Tomorrow would, I hoped, be my last day of novice training, but I still had a lot of work ahead. I tried to forget all that and concentrate instead on the underwater world I had experienced during the last few days – the coral, the fish, the sea . . . And lulled by the rocking of the boat, I fell asleep.

DAY 5

'Hallo, Reg,' I said, handing him a cup of tea in the early-morning sunshine as the *Lady Jenny* bobbed shallowly at anchor.

The scene that greeted me was completely different from the one I'd seen outside my porthole the previous night. Ever since dawn, there had been the rattle and groan of what sounded like miles of anchor cable. Apparently Alex and the engineer Geoff had been grappling with a rather complicated 'Y' mooring to fasten the *Jenny* to her new base.

'This is one of those magic places,' Reg said dreamily, waving his hand towards the high cliffs that rose abruptly out of the water a few hundred metres away. 'Ras Muhammed, one of the best dives in the world.'

The landscape was forbidding: stark cliffs and then miles of barren inhospitable desert. But crystal-clear water lapped invitingly against the prow of the boat, and as I looked down, it seemed to dissolve into a blue nothingness.

Reg was still musing. 'It's beautiful here – it's *always* beautiful here.

Panic stations!

Despite the anxieties of most beginners, who think they're bound to run out of air and be stranded at 30 metres, the chances of ever having to rescue someone underwater – or be rescued yourself – are extremely small. Diving is safe provided you follow the rules and don't take unwarranted risks. However, it's important to know the procedures even though you may never have to use them.

As well as learning how to deal with an unconscious diver – as I'd done with Reg as my willing victim – you should also know how to cope if you or your buddy runs out of air or if he or she gets into some other kind of dangerous situation.

Out of air

You should check your contents

KEY

GUL

Day 5 continued

gauge throughout every dive so that you're always aware of how much air you have left at any particular moment. And, before diving, it's a good idea to decide with your buddy at what point you want to surface – e.g. as you go into the danger zone on your gauge or when a particular amount of air remains.

However, it's not uncommon for divers to run out of air by becoming engrossed in some task – say, photography – and forgetting to check their gauge. Rarely, it can also happen that a fault develops in a demand valve (regulator) and the air supply is slowed down or stops altogether.

If you do begin to run out of air, your demand valve won't suddenly shut off; rather, you will find that it gradually gets harder to breathe. Remember that you will need less air with each breath as you go up, and this will

Day 5 continued

The bottom just drops out of the ocean – it goes straight down. The first part is to about 50 metres, then it jumps and slopes to about 1000.'

The Wall, as it's called, is literally that: a wall that drops away for over half a mile. Reg warned me that it wasn't a place to be without an experienced diver, certainly not at my standard, and that I should never swim deeper than he did.

'You should keep your eye on me the whole time,' he said. 'To emphasize that, we're going to do the last exercise of your course here – the underwater rescue. And I'm not going to tell you when I'm going to do it. Suddenly, I'm just going to need rescuing!'

Great! I thought. *If anyone is going to need rescuing, it's going to be me! However, I suppose it's my duty as a 'buddy' to be lurking if anything goes wrong.*

A delicious smell of toast and fried bacon drifted up to us from the galley where our cook was dishing up to the strains of 'O Sole Mio'. But breakfast was not on Mike's agenda. No time for such frivolities – as far as he was concerned, we were lucky to get a cup of tea.

While we were getting kitted up on the diving deck, Reg explained what the rescue would entail. He was going to throw a wobbly at some point during our dive on The Wall, and I was to bring him to the surface steadily, using his inflated life jacket. Once at the surface, I would give him EAR – expired air resuscitation – by blowing into his nose. Finally, I would hail Tamara, who would be standing by in the Zodiac, by using the wide 'Help!' wave.

So, into our wet suits again, another pre-dive check and – *whoosh!* – into the blue water of the Red Sea for my first sight of The Wall. It was overwhelming; even though the water was virtually transparent, I couldn't see the seabed, just the sheer coral-encrusted

make you feel more comfortable. Signal to your buddy that you're short of air – the clenched fist – and are going up; as long as you've not been down too long at too great a depth, you can ascend steadily without any decompression stops. For example, if you've been down to, say, 30 metres for 20 minutes or less, it will take you about 2 minutes to reach the surface. Your buddy should be with you all the way. Once on the surface, inflate both your life jackets and signal 'Help!' to the boat or shore.

Panic

There are many reasons why a diver, and especially a beginner, might panic, such as running out of air, water conditions (e.g. murky, cold, deep depth), entanglement in seaweed or a fishing net, incorrect buoyancy, a leaky mask. In fact, panic

fore, but not a decompression dive with stops. As we finned along, Reg regularly pointed to my depth and contents gauges, to get me to check our depth and the amount of air left in my cylinder. We were wavering between 9 and 10 metres – just right – and after a time, I found myself checking automatically. It's obviously a drill one gets accustomed to, and after the previous night's lecture on decompression, I could see the point.

The more we dived together, the safer I felt because we were developing a rhythm of safety checks. Passing some coral, we'd linger a

buttress that we were swimming along. It really was quite an extraordinary feeling, knowing that The Wall dropped away to eternity, and I kept glancing towards the surface, afraid that I'd sink deeper and deeper without knowing it.

Reg had told me that we were going to be diving to 10 metres this time – just a little deeper than be-

can result from quite small problems (and ones that should have been dealt with before going down), but underwater, they can seem quite important, even life-threatening.

How will you know that divers are panicking? Probably the first thing you'll notice is that they go into the 'vertical mode' – that is, they 'stand' in the water, with their head towards the surface and their feet towards the seabed, poised for ascent. Their movements will become agitated and they may flap around wildly.

Panic causes divers to breathe heavily and sharply, and you can tell this is happening to other people by the increase in bubbles from their demand valve. This type of breathing will also make them suck on their mouthpiece, and because it was designed primarily to accommodate regular breathing, it won't function well with sharp intakes of breath. This

Day 5 continued

while, investigating all the little nooks and crannies. Then just before we moved off, Reg would pick up his contents gauge, check it, look at his depth gauge, check that, and then look over at me. I'd check mine, and then we'd give each other 'OK' signs – no worries. Diving like this was a cinch.

The coral harboured some of the most beautiful tropical fish I'd ever seen – thousands of small ones buzzing in and out of holes and

crevices, as well as some monsters. Two tunafish came along that must have been 1.5 metres long and, since everything in the water looks a third bigger than it really is, they seemed even more gigantic. Their eyes were huge, and they ogled us closely, completely unintimidated.

At this depth, everything was tinged with the transparent blue of the sea. The vivid colours of both the fish and the coral (particularly the soft kind) only sprang to life

can convince divers that the system isn't working and so compound their anxiety – it's a vicious circle.

It's vitally important to make panicked divers feel secure and return their breathing to normal. Guide them to the bottom or to, say, a rock or reef where they can grab on to something if they feel the need – thrashing about in the open water doesn't promote a feeling of security and well-being!

Watch their breathing for 30 seconds or so. If they relax, the dive can continue; keep making 'OK' signals until you're satisfied that they're calm enough to go on.

If their breathing doesn't improve, signal to them that they should be going up. Keep hold of them as you ascend, letting some air into their life jacket to effect the ascent.

It is quite normal to be anxious on your first five or ten dives, especially if

Day 5 continued

when caught in the artificial light we were using for filming.

Suddenly, I noticed that Reg had stopped moving and was floating awkwardly, his arms and legs flopping in the current. He was obviously taking his acting very seriously.

Help! I thought, and my mind raced as I tried to remember all the heroics that Reg had taught me in the pool. Here, with the bottom of the ocean 1000 metres below, the situation was *very* different. Still, for my first rescue attempt I think I behaved rather valiantly.

With my left hand, I grabbed Reg's jacket and pulled on him so that he was vertical and facing me. Still holding on to him, I then took his direct feed in my other hand and inflated his life jacket by pushing in the air button; not finning at all, we both gently floated to the surface. Although the natural response is to want to get there as quickly as possible, I took care not to let us ascend faster than the regulation 15 metres per minute, by watching the bubbles rise over Reg's shoulder.

When we finally reached the surface, I inflated his life jacket a bit more, and then did the same to mine. This way, we both bobbed about in the choppy current with our heads above water. According to the plan, Reg wasn't supposed to be breathing at this point, so I removed his mouthpiece and mine, and both our masks, and pulled his head right back to open his windpipe. With my other hand, I held his mouth shut by pushing on his chin, and then mimed breathing into his nose through my mouth.

After I'd given him what I reckoned was a decent amount of air, I gave the 'Help' wave – straight arm and a very high, wide movement – and Tamara came racing over in the Zodiac.

'One dead body for you, Tamara!' I shouted above the noise as the inflatable swung round beside us. I

you're going deeper than you have before. Much of this can be avoided if you take your training seriously and learn all the emergency drills thoroughly; in addition, confidence in your instructor is imperative. It is a sad fact that panic is probably the cause of the majority of fatal diving accidents.

In some parts of the world, barracudas are more feared than sharks, despite the fact that attack by barracudas is virtually unknown. Perhaps this is because groups of them will follow divers curiously – a frightening sight with their razor-sharp teeth and cold eyes.

Day 5 continued

reached over and hung on to its side for dear life as Tamara grabbed the jacket of the still-comatose Reg.

'Reg? Reg! You're taking acting too far!' I yelled. 'OK, OK, you've got your Equity card!'

At this, my buddy 'woke up'. 'Well done,' said the newly animated corpse.

'Well done' indeed. During a normal training course, you do the rescue perhaps twice, but we must have done it 18 or 20 times – until Mike was *finally* satisfied. By the end of that session, I could have rescued anybody under the sun. And I think Reg began to wonder whether he really did want to be a film star after all; the prospect of returning to a peaceful life of teaching at the Porchester Baths must have seemed extremely attractive.

By now, we were both exhausted, so we heaved ourselves wearily into Tamara's Zodiac and discarded our equipment.

'How did I really do?' I asked.

'Very well.'

'Passed?'

'Blow in my nose and I'll follow you for ever,' he replied with an impish grin. 'Yes, you've passed.'

'Have I really? So is that all the training done?'

'Just the oral to come.'

'Can't get much more oral than breathing into your nose!'

'We'll finish all your tests tonight.'

'Great!' I was impatient to finish my formal training and get down to some serious sport diving. As we'd had to go over every section of the training a number of times for the filming, I felt fairly confident about taking the oral test now. If I passed, I'd be able to enjoy diving for its own sake and not have to do any more safety drills and exercises. And, while I'd still have to be accompanied by an instructor, I'd also be able to dive with the others on the *Lady Jenny* and wander

The barber shops of the depths

Cooperation between species is not limited to the clownfish and anemones. Many types of smaller wrasse, known collectively as 'cleaner' or 'barber' fish, have created a niche in aquatic society that's unparalleled.

They usually operate in pairs and always stay near their chosen patches of the reef, known as 'cleaning stations'. Larger (and sometimes extremely aggressive) fish will visit them, and make a sign that they require the cleaners' services – for example, the grouper will open its mouth and gills and the goatfish will stand on its head or tail. The cleaner fish will then dart all over them like so many

Day 5 continued

nervous valets, nibbling away the parasites that have become attached to their 'customers'.

Even the most ferocious predators recognize the role of the cleaner fish and will not harm them. The small wrasse can often be seen entering the mouths of normally vicious fish to clean their teeth, emerging unscathed when the job is done.

Another fish – *Aspidontus* – is virtually identical to the cleaner fish, and it will use this uncanny resemblance to lure other fish to come close. When one is within range, it will take a nip from the hoodwinked fish's eye or other soft spot before zipping away.

Day 5 continued

around freely. I was dying to do that.

When we reached the *Jenny*, we handed up our equipment to Alex and headed for the galley for a quick brunch before Mike surfaced and made alternative arrangements. After all our exertions, it was the most wonderful meal ever – French toast made from great slabs of bread dipped into beaten egg and then fried – and we had as much as we could pack in.

You wouldn't think it, but diving makes you incredibly hungry *all the time*. I suppose you must use an awful lot of energy while finning, and staying down for nearly an hour every time you dive must constitute quite a lot of exercise. In fact, Reg later told me that professional divers use up more calories than steel workers!

'By the way,' he mumbled now, his mouth full of toast, 'did I tell you that we were diving under the Shark Observatory?'

'No-oo-oo,' I said doubtfully.

'Yes, it's a platform on top of the crag over there—' he pointed towards the cliffs— 'and people go there to look down and spot sharks. Shame we didn't come across any – they're fascinating.'

I'd already noticed that divers like Reg and Mike rate sharks very highly – they're simply potty about them – and say that they're really nothing to be frightened about. However, having made only a few dives in the open water, I wasn't ready to share their enthusiasm – not just yet. 'Jaws' could wait!

Sharks

Sharks have a special place in the mythology of the sea, and this has been enhanced in the last decade by the *Jaws* series of films, in which a great white shark, with immense cunning and amazing mental powers, attacks and kills everyone in its path.

The reality is a little less dramatic. Of the 250 species of shark, only about 10 are known to have attacked humans. For example, the biggest – the whale shark, which can reach a length of over 18 metres and weigh up to 25 tons – eats only squid, small fish and plankton.

Scientists have placed sharks relatively far down the evolutionary ladder because their skeletons are made up of flexible cartilage, not bone, and because of their small brains. However, this fish has more than made up for these shortcomings by develop-

Day 5 continued

I got out of my wet things and went up to lie on deck, fully intending to do some revising for my oral exam. But then the peace that had enveloped the boat while I lay in the hot sun was disturbed by the appearance of the French divers, all six of them, getting kitted up and doing their pre-dive checks: attaching cylinders, checking depth gauges, sliding their decompression tables in pockets of their wet suits, peering at watches. They were joined by Alex who gave instructions in fractured but impressive French, and then they all climbed down to the Zodiac where Tamara was waiting.

As the inflatable purred away, I tried to concentrate on the sorts of questions that Reg might ask me later, but the slight rolling of the boat and the lull of the waves slapping against the side were too much for me, and I fell into a deep sleep.

After a good dive, all I ever wanted to do was collapse. Being in the water such a lot really relaxes you, soothing every muscle – it must be the best antidote against the rushing around we usually do. This

ing extraordinarily powerful sensory organs, scattered on its head and on the sides of its body, that can perceive even minute changes in its aquatic environment. Among other things, these organs can analyse vibrations and chemicals in the water, and they give the shark information about hydrostatic pressure, sounds (even at ultrasonic levels), odours, etc. It's due to these organs that sharks have their celebrated ability to detect the floundering of wounded animals even at great distances.

You shouldn't, however, lose any sleep over sharks. They're often afraid of divers' exhaust bubbles, they normally feed at night and you're not their natural food. According to Jacques Cousteau, you have about as much chance of being bitten by a shark as being bitten by a dog – and we don't walk around in constant fear of dogs. Feel comforted?

Day 5 continued

therapy of diving, eating and sleeping was absolute bliss.

I was awakened suddenly by a shout, and as I groggily raised myself to a sitting position, I saw Ray looking out over the water and pointing. I turned my head and, as if still dreaming, saw that dolphins were playing all round the boat. Unable to resist this extraordinary opportunity, Ray and some of the others leapt into the Zodiac and took it in among them as they dived and jumped. I'd seen this sort of thing on television but this was the first time I'd ever experienced it myself.

The dolphins were such lovely creatures and really seemed to enjoy all the attention they were getting, showing off like mad – as if they were all desperately auditioning for *The Son of Flipper*! One minute they'd be doing head-stands, waving their tails high in the air for the count of ten, and then, with a lot of little jumps, they'd be diving under the boat again and again.

They were so friendly that we wondered if we could dive with them, but Alex and Tamara told us that we'd only have to put our feet in the water and they'd be off like a shot. But there was no doubt that they enjoyed our company, lingering at a safe distance for about half an hour, certainly long enough for us to use up rolls of film. They were infuriating to photograph: you never knew exactly where they

Sharks have very poor eyesight, and to them, divers look like large seals; luckily, only the great white is interested in them. However, most sharks do go for animals in distress, so a diver flapping about on the surface is in more danger than a submerged one. Even attacks by the great white, the most feared shark, have often been as the result of divers trailing fish they've speared. Resting surfers and windsurfers off the coast of California and on Australia's Great Barrier Reef are in particular danger because, to a shark swimming below, the shape of the surfboard, together with the legs of the surfer hanging over the edge, looks very much like the outline of a stranded seal.

According to a tourist brochure, the last shark attack in the Red Sea where I was diving occurred about 25 years ago. A German girl, a champion swimmer, was on the surface, far out

Day 5 continued

were going to pop up next. What with everyone on board shouting and pointing in different directions at the same time, the photographers among us would invariably run to the wrong side of the boat. Maybe that was all part of the dolphins' fun – I wouldn't be surprised.

They finally left, undoubtedly swimming off to enchant another boatload of admirers. When Ray and the others returned, they were still ecstatic: 'Fabulous!' 'Did you see . . .?' 'What an experience!' Adrian, joining us for a moment, told us that seeing a school of dolphins was a very good omen, but somehow, we already knew that. The wonderful sight of those cavorting animals was just one more episode in a week that, in retrospect, would seem totally unreal – as if we'd been on a different planet most of the time.

As the sun began to go down, Reg and I went back to our favourite spot on deck and settled down for my oral exam. Although this was a serious business – the diving organizations are very strict about novices learning all the basics by heart, like learning the Highway Code for your driving test – I felt fairly relaxed about it, and was quite confident that I would know most of the answers.

'Now,' Reg began, 'what should your normal ascent from a dive be?'

'Um – er – 15 metres a minute,' I responded hesitantly.

'Right. Now let's suppose you're out of sight of the reef or anything else. How on earth would you know how fast 15 metres a minute was?'

'You must never ascend quicker than the small bubbles.'

Then we went on to the underwater hand signals, the ones for 'OK', 'Help!', 'I'm in trouble' and so on.

'How would you signal "I've got no air at all"?' Reg asked.

'If you had no air at all, you would

near some large boats. During their voyages, the crews had thrown the usual refuse overboard, and this had attracted sharks in to their anchorage. Unfortunately, they were also attracted to the German diver, and she lost a leg.

Sharks *are* unpredictable and should always be treated with respect, especially the great white and the hammerhead, the latter being instantly recognizable by its ugly head shaped like a two-headed hammer, its eyes set at the ends of wide 'wings' protruding from it. If a shark is interested in you, it will circle for some time and may even 'taste' you by grazing you with its rough skin. It's good to know, however, that a lot of dramatic film footage of attacking sharks has only been achieved after taunting the animals with blood or dead fish, to make them more aggressive for the camera.

Day 5 continued

make the chopping motion—' I demonstrated— 'wouldn't you?'

'That's right – like being chopped off at the throat . . . Now let's think about something else: burst lung. That sounds a pretty terrible thing to suffer from. How might you get burst lung?'

'If you ascend and you hold your breath at the same time, the air in your lungs will expand and this could injure you.'

Reg really took me through my paces that evening, questioning me on everything he had told me in the lectures. He asked me about pre-dive checks, how an aqualung works, the different ways you can clear your ears while diving and other important safety matters.

Then he said: 'Let's start dealing with the question of deeper diving now, Annie. What happens to your body when you dive deep for a relatively long time?'

I explained how the various gases in the air – mainly oxygen and nitrogen – gradually seep into the bloodstream, but while oxygen is used by the body, the nitrogen isn't and can cause trouble when you ascend, such as the bends.

'What can you do to avoid decompression sickness?'

'You should use the tables, which tell you how long you can stay on the bottom without getting into trouble.'

'That's right, but don't forget that they also tell you how long and at what depth you have to make decompression stops.' Reg now gave me a decompression table. 'Let's see if you know how to use one of these. Say you've been diving at 40 metres for 20 minutes. For how long and at what depth would you have to make a decompression stop?'

I looked down the table and found the answer (it was amazing how easy it was to use now): 'Five minutes at 10 metres and ten minutes at 5 metres!'

'Right! You've really learned that

Here are a few tips on how to behave if you meet a shark:

- Stay calm. Sharks are attracted to animals in distress.
- Don't rush to the surface.
- Calmly swim away.
- If possible, get close to another diver. The shark, with its poor vision, will think you're one big fish rather than two small ones.
- If you're in open water, swim to a reef.

Dolphins

These are some of the best-loved animals in the world, due to their immense sense of fun and to the peculiar caring attitude they have towards humans, even when hunted by these non-aquatic 'friends'.

Dolphins are classified in the same mammal group – the cetaceans – as whales and porpoises. While they resemble the latter, porpoises are well. Now, what are the effects of nitrogen narcosis?'

'Um, probably the same sort of symptoms that some people on the boat have in the evening – drunk and disorderly!'

'You're not far wrong there.'

The subject of nitrogen narcosis had become, despite its potential seriousness, a standing joke on the *Lady Jenny*. Everyone seemed to be suffering from 'the narcs' every night from about nine o'clock on – strange, considering nobody had been diving particularly deeply . . . As if on cue, while I ran through the specific symptoms for Reg, I could hear evidence of all the sure signs – drunkenness, wooziness, inability to concentrate, euphoria – wafting up from the deck below where Adrian's barbecue was well under way.

That was the last question; the exam was over.

With a smile, Reg told me that I'd passed my oral with flying colours.

While he'd been testing me, the sun had dipped below the horizon. In these parts, when the sun sets, it gets quite cool very quickly, even though it may have been in the 80s only a matter of minutes before.

The coming of night had another effect, an unfortunate one for me and the film crew. Mike had been

actually smaller and less extrovert and don't have the toothed 'beak' of the dolphins.

All spring from a common ancestor, the same one as terrestrial carnivores. However, unlike these land-based mammals, the cetaceans returned to the sea where (although they, too, are surface-breathing) they live continuously – not even coming on to land to breed or give birth.

When a dolphin is born (after a gestation of 10–12 months, and then, tail first), the mother is assisted by another female – a 'midwife'. Other dolphins in the school, which can sometimes number over 1000, crowd around to protect the mother and baby from sharks, which would be attracted to the blood in the water. After the baby is born, the mother pushes it to the surface so it can take its first breath. Dolphins also do this if one of their species is wounded, and

Day 5 continued

filming during the oral test – a lovely picture of Reg and me in silhouette against the sea and sky ablaze with the setting sun. He'd obviously miscalculated how long it would take because, before we were even half finished, the sun went down! Time waits for no man, not even Mike, and now he announced that, to complete the shot, we'd all have to get up at *five o'clock* the next morning, to film against the *rising* sun! Hopefully, this would match what he'd just been shooting.

There was nothing for it but to drown our sorrows and get well narc'd with the rest. The French were already well stuck in by the time we joined them – they had got to the maudlin-sea-shanty-singing stage. The song was something about a sardine and had a very catchy chorus involving lots of *ho-ho-ho's*, but we were a bit dubious about the bits in between that drew a great deal of raucous laughter from the French quarter.

The spread that arrived from both the barbecue and the *Jenny*'s tiny galley was fabulous, particularly the lovely fresh tuna, and it was all washed down with what seemed like gallons of wine. It was therefore a merry crowd that Alex tried to subdue.

'Quiet, quiet, everybody, *please*,' he said patiently, 'let's have a little bit of hush.' He finally got everybody's attention. 'We've got some very good news this evening. Reg has told me that Anneka, who's been training with him, has at last passed her novice diver's test!'

Everybody cheered as I bowed and beamed, feeling rather pleased with myself.

'And in the time-honoured tradition of this vessel,' Alex continued, 'we would like to make our own award . . .'

To my absolute horror, he and Adrian walked over, deftly picked me up and promptly threw me overboard! Unfair!

have even been known to push humans to the surface in just this way.

If you see one in the wild, it is likely to be the common, or saddleback, dolphin, which ranges across the temperate and tropical seas. It can reach up to 2.5 metres in length and is rather slender; dark skinned above and white below, it also has an elaborate pattern of light and dark bands and yellow colouring on its sides. It is capable of speeds of up to 25 knots (about 30 mph), frequently rides bow waves and can make spectacular leaps out of the water.

The ones usually found in aquariums and 'dolphinaria' are bottle-nosed dolphins, which grow to about 3.6 metres and have a distinctive 'beak' and prominent dorsal fin. These have a highly developed social life; intelligent and easily tamed, they can be taught to fetch and carry objects, and other such tricks.

Day 5 continued

When I finally surfaced to a chant of 'Anneka, Anneka . . .' – the French were thoroughly enjoying the spectacle – I couldn't believe what had happened. I seemed to be spending my entire diving trip getting wet, drying off, then getting wet again etc., etc., and an unscheduled and unnecessary soaking late at night was definitely not required!

As I mounted the ladder, a sea of hands reached down to help me and someone threw me a towel. I was led triumphantly back to the table where I was cheered with another glass of wine – purely medicinal, of course.

What *did* dampen my spirits, though, was the thought of the obscenely early start the next day. We all soon made our farewells and turned in for the night, Ray as usual heading for a quiet part of the deck to sleep under the stars.

I was only dimly aware that I was crawling into bed – it had been a busy day – but as I tried to find a patch of pillow that hadn't become sodden from my wet hair, I had the uninspiring thought that I'd be getting up again in a few hours. Tomorrow was going to be different, though – no more training, no more tests. I was now a qualified novice diver and could bravely go where no man had been before. The only blot on the horizon was 5.00 a.m.

DAY 6

A timid knock on my cabin door developed into a loud thumping as Mike realized that half-hearted attempts were not going to get me anywhere near the sunrise that morning. It was still dark, my eyes refused to open and I decided, then and there, to get a nine-to-five job when I got back home.

When I finally crawled up on deck, Reg was looking remarkably wide awake. As we settled down to relive my oral exam, Mike and the rest of the crew tried to set up the equipment around the motionless lump that was Ray – his 'bedroom' on deck was our set.

This 'day for night' stuff is a real trick of the trade. The rising sun can look just as if it's setting; the early morning sea can look every bit as romantic and tranquil as it does in the evening. It's the *human* factor that's the problem, when you're still half asleep, dry-throated and baggy-eyed – thank God, Mike had decided to shoot all this in silhouette!

Qualifying tests

As well as satisfying your instructor that you have all the theory of diving down pat, you must pass various tests in the water before you become qualified as a Novice or Sports Diver. (There are even more stringent tests to qualify as a Dive Leader, Advanced Diver, First-Class diver and Instructor.)

During my training in the Red Sea, I qualified as a British Sub-Aqua Club Novice Diver and made some dives that will go towards my Sports Diving qualification. On the next two pages you can see what it involved.

Sports diver

- All the rescue skills listed are tested at a depth of 5 metres. When rescuing your buddy, you also

Day 6 continued

Still, by the time I had about a gallon of black coffee inside me, the bright morning sunshine had revived me, though not Ray, who slept through the entire proceedings. Oh well, you can't expect a photographer to know where the action is . . .

Eventually, Reg and I relived the previous night's test to Mike's satisfaction – which meant I'd finished my novice diving course, both on and off camera.

Passing my test didn't mean that I could now do whatever I wanted. Although I could dive with the others on board and more for pleasure than instruction, I still had to be paired off specifically with Reg, Alex or Tamara.

I was now at the stage that a lot of divers reach: any time I'm on holiday near some interesting water, I'm qualified to go diving as long as I'm accompanied by a dive 'leader' or instructor. And most people are happy to leave their qualifications at that. However, if you want to progress to the level where you can be in charge of a dive and are therefore that much more independent, there is a whole range of tests to take and of qualifying dives to be notched up.

For example, we were diving on The Wall that morning because some of the divers on the boat wanted Reg to test them for their dive-leader exam. They needed to go to certain depths and perform drills and exercises as part of their training, to prove to him that they were competent and responsible. The French divers, on the other hand, were so experienced that, before each dive, Alex and Tamara only had to go through their dive plan with them and tell them about the particular coral reef they were going to be diving in; then they were quite happy to let them go off and enjoy their dive and exploration on their own.

It was another sunny day, but it

have to remove unwanted equipment; tow him 50 metres to safety, giving regular EAR; assist in his removal from the water on to the shore, and provide basic aftercare.

- One snorkel swim lasting at least 30 minutes – of 300 metres, with dives up to a depth of 5 metres.
- 10 qualifying dives, each of at least 15 minutes' duration and totalling not less than 3 hours underwater. These must be made at various sites involving different conditions and activities, and include at least 5 of the following:

(1) shore dive along shelving bottom
(2) dive from small boat
(3) dive in freshwater
(4) dive in moving water (1 knot maximum)
(5) dive in seawater.
(6) limited visibility dive (approx. 2 metres)
(7) dive in cold water (10°C or less)
(8) dive to 25 metres

Day 6 continued

Practical tests of the British Sub-Aqua Club

PURPOSE
While under training, a trainee should only progress to new or more complex skills after basic ones have been mastered. In effect, each lesson serves as a test in which a satisfactory standard must be reached in order for the trainee to embark on the next.

However, on completion of all training, set tests serve as a means of assessing whether all practical training objectives have been reached and go a long way towards achieving uniform standards throughout the Club. For these reasons, the Novice Diver course includes obligatory tests which relate to and endeavour to simulate both routine and emergency diving practices.

CONDUCT
Trainees should not be put forward for tests until their instructor considers them to be ready and in possession of the necessary levels of skill and stamina.

All tests must be undertaken as a continuous activity with no significant rest pauses between each part. Trainees should be briefed accordingly; examiners should ensure no rests are taken. No minimum time limits are imposed on any of these tests, but if trainee's have difficulty in carrying out tests as a continuous activity, this could indicate a lack of general stamina which might be grounds for failure.

In particular, this applies to the Basic Skills Test — Part 1. This test has been deliberately designed to assess stamina, and the NDC suggests that a trainee's stamina should be questioned if he takes more than 25 minutes to complete this test.

When conducting tests, persons acting as examiners should have the relevant training objectives in mind and should judge the effectiveness of the trainee's technique rather than the precision of the performance.

BASIC SKILLS TEST
Taken on completion of Skill Groups up to and including NS 5.

Part 1
Trainees are expected to complete Part 1 within 20-25 minutes.

(a) Sink mask, fins and snorkel tube in 2-3m depth of water: dive to recover, and fit at surface.
(b) Fin 200m, including 8 surface dives in appropriate depths.
(c) Fin 50m without mask, face submerged, breathing through snorkel.
(d) Fin 50m on back, with mask and snorkel removed.
(e) Fin underwater for a distance of not less than 15m.
(f) Fin 100m on surface, wearing 5kg weightbelt.

Part 2
To be performed in a buddy pair with another trainee.
As far as possible, buddy diving practices should be observed throughout this test.

(a) Assemble and test aqualung and put it on.
(b) Conduct equipment check and buddy check with diving buddy.
(c) Enter water (depth 2-3m), demonstrate neutral buoyancy within normal range of breathing.
(d) Remove mask, replace and clear. Repeat twice.
(e) Release mouthpiece, recover, replace and clear. Repeat twice.
(f) Surface from 2-3m using correct surfacing drill. Fit snorkel, give 'OK' Signal. Repeat twice.
(g) Give 'OK' and 'descend' signals: make descent with buddy.
(h) Share aqualung at depth 2-3m. From 5m distance, approach buddy who is signalling 'I have no more air'. Establish breathing exchange rhythm, then fin 25m horizontally while sharing. Perform once as a donor of air, once as a receiver of air.
(i) Fin 50m under water with blacked-out mask, led by buddy, or following tiles, rope, etc.
(j) While treading water, remove weightbelt and pass up to poolside, remove aqualung and pass up to poolside. Leave water at the same point (assistance permitted).
(k) Wash down and dismantle aqualung set.

Day 6 continued

ABLJ & Rescue Skills Test

Taken on completion of Skill Groups up to and including NS 7.
To be performed in a buddy pair with another trainee. As far as possible, buddy diving practices should be observed throughout this test.

(a) Prepare, assemble and test aqualung and ABLJ/BC. Put them on.

(b) Conduct equipment check and buddy check with diving buddy.

(c) At depth of 2-3m (and with extra weight if necessary) use ABLJ/BC inflation and control to demonstrate buoyancy compensation, and neutral buoyancy by hovering clear of the bottom.

(d) Ascend to surface by means of inflated ABLJ/BC, maintaining slow ascent by fine control of ABLJ/BC venting systems.

(e) Wearing aqualung and ABLJ/BC and approaching from 10m distance, fin at speed to buddy who is simulating unconsciousness on the bottom. Bring buddy to surface in a controlled manner, provide surface buoyancy by inflation of buddy's ABLJ/BC.

(f) Extend buddy's airway, apply simulated EAR. Summon help. Continue to provide support and EAR for 3 minutes.

(Parts (e) and (f) to be performed with a realistic sense of urgency).

Full Equipment Test

Taken on completion of Skill Groups up to and including NS 8.
To be performed in a buddy pair with another trainee. As far as possible, buddy diving practices should be observed throughout this test. Full open water diving equipment to be worn.

(a) Assemble and test aqualung and ABLJ/BC. Put on all equipment without assistance. Adjust harnesses, etc.

(b) Conduct equipment check and buddy check with diving buddy.

(c) Enter water (depth 2-3m), demonstrate neutral buoyancy within normal range of breathing.

(d) Remove mask, replace and clear. Repeat twice.

(e) Release mouthpiece, recover, replace and clear. Repeat twice.

(f) Share aqualung at depth of 2-3m. From 5m distance, approach buddy who is signalling 'I have no more air.' Establish breathing exchange rhythm, then fin 25m horizontally while sharing. Perform once as donor of air, once as receiver of air.

(g) At depth of 2-3m (and with extra weight if necessary) use ABLJ/BC inflation and control to demonstrate buoyancy compensation, and neutral buoyancy by hovering clear of the bottom.

(h) Ascend to surface by means of inflated ABLJ/BC, maintaining slow ascent by fine control of ABLJ/BC venting systems.

(i) Approaching from 10m distance, fin at speed to buddy who is simulating unconsciousness. Bring buddy to surface in a controlled manner, provide surface buoyancy by inflation of buddy's ABLJ/BC.

(j) Extend buddy's airway, apply simulated EAR. Summon help. Continue to provide support and EAR for 3 minutes.

(k) While treading water or supported by ABLJ/BC, remove weightbelt and pass up to poolside, remove aqualung and pass up to poolside. Leave water at the same point (assistance permitted).

(Parts (i) and (j) to be performed with a realistic sense of urgency.)

Day 6 continued

had become terribly windy. Alex told us that, the week before, there'd been Force 8 gales, but it takes more than a bit of wind to deter a diver. Quite a swell had developed, too. This meant that Adrian wouldn't be able to get the *Lady Jenny* near enough to where he wanted to dive, so we were going in from the Zodiac.

As we were getting ready, Alex (who was to be my buddy for the morning) briefed me about our Wall dive. When the sea's rough, it's always much calmer – and therefore safer – just *under* the surface, so we agreed that the moment we rolled in backwards off the side of the Zodiac, we would wait just below the waves until we were both ready to dive deeper. Apparently, being bucketed around on top when it's rough is notoriously dangerous for beginners: there's a great temptation to take out your mouthpiece to speak to your buddy, or to pull up your mask, leaving yourself wide open to a wave slapping you right in the face.

As the Zodiac zipped us over to the portion of the reef where we were to dive, we had to hang on

tightly so that the choppy waves wouldn't throw us out. At first, I was hesitant about rolling backwards off the Zodiac. When we'd practised entering the water at the

Rapture of the depths

Nitrogen is not only responsible for decompression sickness; it's also the culprit in nitrogen narcosis – what that romantic Frenchman, Jacques Cousteau, called *'l'ivresses des grandes profondeurs'*, or rapture of the depths. (The less poetic divers of the Royal Navy refer to it as 'the narcs'!)

Nitrogen narcosis is the antithesis of panic, but it can be just as dangerous. Instead of flailing around wildly, mind clouded by fear, the diver suffering from nitrogen narcosis feels a totally unfounded sense of well-being, mental confusion, a loss of all sense of time passing and, in some cases, tunnel vision.

The dangers can be imagined. If a dive is to be a safe one, absolute attention must be paid to bottom time, depth, decompression stops and many other vital details. Swanning

Day 6 continued

pool at Eilat, I'd had no trouble with the step entry. I just took a deep breath and, with only slight apprehension, stepped off the edge and plunged in. However, when it came to rolling backwards, I kept imagining that I would roll right round and hit my head on the side of the pool.

It's easy to build up mental blocks about things, and the *thought* of rolling backwards into the water, virtually upside down, *was* off-putting. But, in reality, the sides of the Zodiac were like huge cushions, and I was so close to the sea that it would be like rolling out of bed! The only thing I had to remember was to hold on to my mask, so that it wouldn't slip off as I hit the water. By the time I'd watched as the French divers flopped, one by one, into the water like seals, it was obviously no big deal – and I was looking forward to that delicious feeling of being back underwater.

It was, thankfully, much calmer

and smoother as I hovered just a few feet beneath the waves and, viewed from underneath, the surface looked like shaken sheets of silk.

The shots we were doing now – general cutaway shots – would be

about in deep water with a silly grin on your face is not the answer.

Nitrogen narcosis affects divers more the deeper they swim, with the major onset occurring at about 40 metres, and it's also more likely to occur in beginners and even in the more experienced who have not dived for some time. Although the depth at which a person is affected depends very much on the individual, the Americans have devised what they call 'Martini's law': this equates every 10 metres of a dive with the intoxication produced by drinking one martini. Nitrogen narcosis is also known as 'depth drunkenness'!

To avoid it, all divers should follow the most basic rule of the sport: *never dive alone*. The only advantage of nitrogen narcosis over decompression sickness is that its effects disappear when you make your ascent; there is no sickness and no hangover.

Day 6 continued

slotted in at various points in the final film. And here I really had trouble with continuity, mainly because I'd been foolish enough to choose those two masks, one white and the other pink. I had to take both down with me and try to communicate with Mike underwater: 'Is this the shot where I had the watch on and the pink mask, or the white mask and the gloves?' Never again – from now on, I'll always wear the same things!

And, of course, changing masks underwater meant a lot of mask clearing, which I didn't like at all. I'd vaguely hoped that Mike would allow me to swim to the surface to do this – but I should have known better than even to contemplate wasting so much valuable filming time!

The water here was still astonishingly clear, and with the coral illuminated by the lights that Graham held for Mike's underwater photography, it was like an enchanted forest. Reg had told me that, for him, the sensation of being underwater was sometimes like being in a dream, and here at South Reef, I knew what he meant.

It was a new experience, diving with Alex, but I came to feel just as safe and reassured with him as I had with Reg. Alex, too, kept a very close eye on me, especially at the

Day 6 continued

beginning of our dive, continually turning to me to check that I was all right until he was satisfied that I was happy and comfortable. It was quite interesting to learn the routine of another diver, reading his facial expressions, noticing when he was trying to draw my attention to something specific or maybe laughing together.

I was glad to have another chance to investigate this famous Wall, and found that it retained its fascination – it was amazing how there was always something new to see within its crevices and clinging to it. In the light of Alex's torch, the colours of the soft corals (a brilliant orange) and the delicacy of the coral fans simply took my breath away. We dallied here and there, peering into little holes on the cliffside, disturbing the inmates to see what else might be lurking there. Everything I touched had a different texture: hard, soft, spiny, smooth.

Day 6 continued

As we rounded a corner of this underwater coral cliff, Alex waved his hand to make me look down. I took one look and then quickly swam closer to him and to The Wall; below us was the darkest, deepest blue I'd ever seen, stretching away to infinity. I didn't think I suffered from vertigo, but I had a taste of it then – a slightly sickening, dizzy feeling.

Mike was very keen to get a shot of us as tiny pinpricks against the huge scale of The Wall, and as Alex and I swam along it, with our director and his camera some distance away, I felt quite diminished. It really brought home to me that we were like a pair of tiny birds flying beside this massive cliff with the yawning abyss below.

However, Alex was by my side, and I controlled my anxiety by using common sense: I checked my contents gauge (I still had loads of air left), checked our depth (20 metres), took a few steady, deep breaths and felt fine again. I just decided not to look down for a while . . .

By now, I'd got my buoyancy just right. If I paused for a second, I would hang there in the water, just like the fish I so admired. Then, if I saw something interesting above me, I knew that all I had to do was inhale and I'd rise like some pantomime Peter Pan! And if I saw an interesting crop of coral below me, I'd flip upside down, exhale and just sink down to it – absolute magic!

(Even as I'm writing this, I still marvel at the sensation of diving and the unique experience it gives you of being like another species. I can't even bear to think about it – I wish I were there *now*!)

At the end of my longest and somehow most *serious* dive so far, Alex and I surfaced about the same time as the French. As we all struggled out of our wet suits back on the *Lady Jenny*, I joined in the chatter about what we'd all seen. I felt quite the veteran.

The dive-boat routine was quite a rigmarole, but I was beginning to get the hang of it now. First, we all had to store our personal diving equipment – demand valves, snorkels, masks, fins, depth gauges – in our own crates, stowing these away on the dive deck. Then we had to

Day 6 continued

take our empty tanks round to the side of the boat near to the compressor, ready for Alex to refill. After that, we had to rinse out our wet suits and hang them up anywhere we could find a space. And then, at last, we could rush to grab a place at the breakfast table.

Yes, all that (*and* the sunrise shoot) and we still hadn't had any breakfast! Even so, I loved those early-morning dives. The guests on the boat would always try to fit in a dive before 8.00 a.m. so that they could really appreciate the feast of a breakfast served at about 9.00. However, as I've said before, the film crew and I rarely experienced this phenomenon called 'food'!

Later in the morning, there was time for a few hours' serious sunbathing or napping in the shade. Once you're up to the full complement of three long dives a day – and because of the filming, I was in the water even more – not only does the exercise tire you out, but all that nitrogen floating around in your

Day 6 continued

bloodstream definitely has a soporific effect. Besides, to keep within the safety margins of the BSAC tables, you should ideally wait about six hours between dives, especially if they're deep ones. For the same reason, Alex and Tamara always organized the dives so that the deepest ones were done first thing.

Tamara was going to accompany me on my second dive of the day – to Anemone City, somewhere below us at Ras Muhammed. By the size of our entourage of underwater photographers, this was obviously one for the cameras. Mike and Ray came, of course, but also Alex and two of the French diving doctors. I got the feeling that we were in for one of the prettier dives.

Anemone City, to the east of The Wall, *was* beautiful, glowing with thousands of tiny, brightly coloured fish swimming among the swaying fronds of the most exotic anemones I'd ever seen. Each thick mass of tentacles seemed more luscious and more fantastic than the last, and every clump was guarded by its own army of darting clownfish, which cheekily attempted to be menacing by making little thrusts at us. It really was quite comical the way all two inches of them would bravely charge at our inquisitive fingers. As long as we remained re-

Squid

I would imagine that, like me, many people associate squid with terrifying images of the enormous one that tore into Captain Nemo's submarine in Jules Verne's *20,000 Leagues Under the Sea*. And it is true that giant squid can grow up to 20 metres long – almost equalling the size of that other giant of the oceans, the sperm whale. In fact, since the squid plays a significant role in the whale's diet, the two can come into conflict – scientists have found huge sucker scars on whales' tough skin.

While you won't run into any giant squid when you go diving – they inhabit the virtually sunless regions 1000 metres down – the smaller varieties are fairly widespread. They are some of the most intelligent of the

Day 6 continued

tacles with my gloved hands to see the clownfish sheltering there, and then compared the reality with the picture in the book. Then, as I sat calmly on a rock, reading about all the exotic fish shown on the pages, it was as if someone had suddenly shouted, 'Cue fish!': just as I was examining the picture of one particular brightly coloured fish, its

latively still, the anemones simply regarded us as prey: Tamara showed me that, if you stuck a pencil among their fronds, they would wrap themselves around it and tug rather futilely.

The little clownfish were a delight, and I wanted to know more about them. I looked at Tamara questioningly. She obligingly produced a rather ingenious *waterproof* reference book with pages and pages of photographs of all the fish surrounding us, which were accompanied by explanatory captions.

I peered into a sea anemone, brushing back its poisonous ten-

invertebrates, having a simple brain that consists of several masses of nerve tissue arranged around the gullet between the eyes; in other invertebrates, this tissue is spread throughout the body. Squid also have a number of exceptionally large nerve cells – called *giant fibres* – which researchers make great use of when studying the physiology of nerves.

In addition, squid have quite powerful sense organs, able to detect chemical changes and to determine balance. But their most significant sense organs are their eyes, which uncannily resemble those of humans and other vertebrates. Like ours, they contain a cornea, lens and retina (the light-sensitive part), but amazingly, the squid developed these along a completely different evolutionary path. Their eyes also operate dif-

Day 6 continued

double swam right over it! At that moment, Mike and his ability to handle extras rose in my estimation by 1000 per cent . . .

Sometimes the fish appeared to be just as curious about us as we were about them. Occasionally, they came right up to the face plate of my mask and took a good look inside, making me squint with the effort of keeping them in focus.

Well, that was enough clowning around for one dive. Tamara looked meaningfully at her contents gauge and made the ascent sign with her thumb. Glancing at my gauge, I was amazed to find that I was already on reserve, with only about five minutes of air left. That's another thing that surprised me: air consumption varies quite a lot depending on the depth (you need more the deeper you go), and from diver to diver and from dive to dive.

For example, you might think that a large man like Reg would consume much more air than a sleek, svelte athlete like me (all right, all right – but it is *my* book), but not so. Reg used up to 30 per cent less air than I would on the same dives. This was particularly true in the early days, because my anxiety made me breathe more frequently and unnecessarily deeply, whereas an old campaigner like Reg is used to

ferently: instead of the lens changing shape to focus, as it does in the human eye, in the squid it is the whole body of the eye that changes, bringing the retina closer to or further away from the lens.

Because of their refined senses and relatively powerful brains, squid have, unlike most marine species, the ability to learn. This is vital since they must somehow outwit their chosen prey – e.g. crabs and lobsters – which are armed and very strong, using their tentacles, complete with suckers, to grab their victims and stuff them in between their jaws. The two longest tentacles are kept partially retracted until a likely subject swims within reach; then, in a flash, they shoot out to capture it.

The squid's mantle provides it with respiration and jet propulsion. Com-

Day 6 continued

breathing just the minimum *and* he expended much less energy by containing his movements.

Because I'd developed a more streamlined mode of propulsion, using my fins alone, I was using much less air than I had just a few days before. But I was still using more than Tamara, which made me wonder at the size of her lungs . . . She's been diving so much that she's probably beginning to develop gills!

Logbook in hand, I was about to join Reg on deck, when I bumped into Ray loading his cameras. 'I didn't have a chance to tell you,' he said, 'but yesterday I felt the early effects of nitrogen narcosis.'

'You and everybody else on the boat last night!' I said.

'No, no, I mean for *real*, when we were diving quite deep.'

'Really?' I exclaimed. I knew that the 'rapture of the depths' (I love that name) was a relatively common occurrence – in *and* out of the water – but I couldn't wait to hear a first-hand account of it happening during a dive. 'What was it like?'

'Frankly, I felt great – but that's what was frightening! I was lulled into this very safe feeling, and became quite light-headed, almost as if I were drunk! I really had to pull myself together. There I was, swimming happily along The Wall with *nothing* below me, and when I realized that, I almost panicked. Luckily, Alex was with me and he got me up to the surface when he saw what was happening. It must have been the stupid grin on my face!'

'Any hangover?'

'Oh no, I feel fine.'

Reg beckoned me from the other side of the deck. As I joined him, I remembered how we'd joked about nitrogen narcosis; Ray had certainly made me aware of how serious it really could be.

'How are you getting on with Alex and Tamara?' Reg asked.

prising a large proportion of its body, this muscle surrounds a water-filled cavity; when the mantle pumps, water is forced out over the gills, where the oxygen is extracted, and when the pumping is pronounced, a stream of water leaves the cavity by way of a siphon and the animal scoots away. Because the siphon can be turned to any angle, the squid can steer itself in any direction it pleases.

Day 6 continued

'It's really weird diving with someone else, having got so used to you. But because the hand signals are so universal, after a while I forgot you weren't with me – sorry!'

'Did you remember your bottom times and all that?'

'Yes, I got that right for once. Tamara was *very* impressed. Actually, I was just going to fill in my logbook now. Should I carry on doing this even though I've finished my novice training?'

'Yes,' he replied, 'logbooks are very important. You may never do dives like these again, and because they're so interesting, you should record them. And, if you are going to carry on with your sport diving —' I nodded enthusiastically— 'I'll move some of the dives you've done here across into your blue BSAC logbook, as qualifying dives.'

'Really? Will some of them count?'

'Yes, so it's important that you note down everything you've done. Then, in the future, you can get a big logbook, stick photos in it and it will become a souvenir, of general interest as well as an official record of your dives.'

During a night dive, it can be difficult to signal to your buddy using hand signals, although officially you are supposed to make these in the beam of your torch.

Instead, you can try to improvise some signals using the torch itself. For example, circling the beam of the torch could mean 'OK' when you're underwater; on the surface, 'OK' could be the slow movement of the beam up and down. For 'Help!' underwater, you could switch the beam on and off; on the surface, you could swing the torch from side to side to mean the same thing.

Whether you're using your torch to signal or just to look around, *never* shine it in another diver's eyes.

Day 6 continued

(Reg was right. Now that I've been diving for some time, I find it fascinating to look back over my log-book. It acts as a cross between a diary and a photo album and is invaluable as a reference book.)

As I wrote down the location, depth and bottom time of the Anemone City dive, the cuts on my hands began to ache. I hadn't been wearing gloves for a lot of the time (a sin according to some authorities), and as a consequence, my hands had been badly scraped and cut by the coral I'd been handling, some of which can slice through the thickest wet suit. Although it's a commonly held belief that the saltiness of the sea acts as a disinfectant, the opposite is true: seawater contains enough 'wildlife' to infect even the smallest cut. So I had to apply a special ointment to all my scrapes and cuts to avoid this. Despite the state of my hands, however, I think I gained a lot by being able to touch so many things down there, adding another dimension to the whole experience.

As the last rays of the sun lit the deck of the *Lady Jenny*, a few of the French divers returned from a dive.

Sea turtles

Lumbering on land but gliding in the sea, sea turtles are an example of how different an animal can appear when seen in its proper environment.

The one we caught on camera was a green turtle, one of the largest of the marine species. These average about 65 kilograms, although one was recorded as having achieved the magnificent weight of over 360 kilograms. This is even more amazing when you consider that these animals are solely plant eaters.

Unlike their terrestrial cousins, the sea turtles have relatively streamlined shells and paddle-like limbs instead of feet, which increase their mobility in water. They have a low metabolic rate and so don't require much oxygen – proportionate to their size, they use 300–400 times less oxygen than humans! – and can therefore

Day 6 continued

The rest of us, however, were getting ready for the night dive. Soon, with no lights on the shore and no pollution in the air to reflect any light from the boat, the sea and sky were swallowed up in utter blackness. I couldn't say that I was looking forward to this.

Alex called us to attention and made sure that each of us knew who our diving partners were. 'Just to remind everybody, there are things that bite and sting around the reef at night. You need to be very careful where you put your hands, where you sit and where you put your knees. Don't start grabbing out into the darkness – you don't really know what you're going to grab! Now let's get into the water and enjoy ourselves, shall we?'

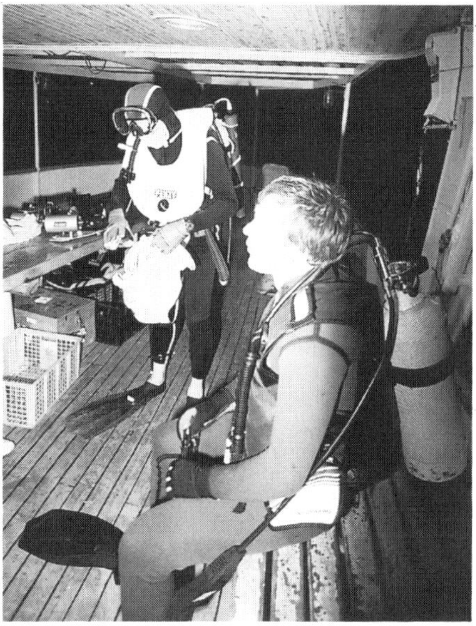

Shall we? I mentally echoed, but I tried to hide my trepidation with a nervous smile. I couldn't suppress a grin, however, when one of the French divers, a woman, announced, 'The Froggies are ready!' Then, one by one, we plunged into the black, black water.

Adrian had directed a powerful spotlight from the top of the *Lady Jenny* to illuminate the area we were going to explore. Despite this, as the others swam off ahead of us, all I could see of them were the turquoise traces of their torches,

spend long periods under water.

The only time they emerge from the sea is to breed and lay their eggs, about 100 at a time. These are not hard-shelled like birds' eggs, but leathery and tough. After about ten weeks' incubation in the sand above the high-water mark, the eggs hatch and baby turtles emerge that are tiny replicas of their parents. If they hatch at night, they have a good chance of making it to the sea and survival. However, if they hatch during the day, they are likely to fall prey to thousands of birds hovering over the beach, waiting for this special delicacy.

While the sight of this seaside slaughter can be particularly gruesome, at least this turtle culling is part of Nature's grand plan. What has made the green turtle an endangered species is not, however, natural: it is the hunting of these animals for their eggs, shells, oil and meat – by hu-

GUL

Day 6 continued

streaking ahead and to the sides. I'm not afraid of the dark, but it was unnerving to be surrounded by such impenetrable blackness, not knowing what was behind me and only able to see what was in the path of my torchlight. Luckily Alex came quickly to my side and turned on his more powerful light.

Diving to between 18 and 22 metres to explore a couple of coral outcrops, our torches acted as magic wands, strips of vivid colour appearing out of the murkiness as we swung them round. This was definitely science-fiction time – the beams from our torches could have been lasers, making some of the night creatures blink and retreat, stunned by the glare during their night-time prowl.

I flinched a bit as I saw just how many gigantic black sea urchins had suddenly appeared in every crevice of the coral, their poisonous quills at least a foot long. The strangest things were the sleeping fish. This was a new one on me. You hear about horses sleeping while they're standing up (I've often wondered if they really do), but this was ridiculous; all these semi-comatose fish parked under sheltering coral. However, with their eyes wide open, it was only their lack of movement that told us that they were dreaming. Alex showed me how to stroke them as they slept – the liberties divers take!

As we finned slowly in the darkness, we came across a squid, at first floating motionless, one of its large, almost-human eyes staring, unblinking, at these two strange fish

mans. In the 250 million years of the turtles' history, they have been reduced from 24 to 11 major types, and the disappearance of different species has accelerated acutely in recent times. It is heartbreaking to think that, some day soon, other divers may be deprived of the experience of seeing a green turtle, its bulk magically transformed into sleekness and manoeuvrability, swimming placidly in the darkness of a coral reef.

There are more than 100 species of surgeonfish (also known as doctorfish), all of which have one thing in common. Right in front of their tails, on both sides, are one or two extremely sharp spines – the surgeon's 'scalpels' – which are capable of giving the unwary diver a deep, but non-poisonous cut. Surgeonfish are usually dark blue or green, though they can suddenly turn white.

Day 6 continued

approaching. Then it darted off into the gloom, propelling itself with a jet of water from inside. While it obviously wasn't a giant squid, it still brought back memories of *20,000 Leagues Under the Sea*.

Fortunately, night turned into day (well, a very foggy day) when the full lighting rig was turned on – a veritable cast of thousands holding up all the lights, and cables snaking all about. Filming in this situation proved to be quite challenging. Mike had made us memorize all his directions beforehand because, once we dived in, we couldn't see anything but the very broadest of gestures in the gloom, and those were only visible because Mike wore a luminous band strapped to his wrist. We had to remember 'First, go left to right. Next shot, go right to left, pause, then swim over camera' and so on, as Mike waved his orange-glowing arm to cue us.

Suddenly he gesticulated wildly, but it took some time before I realized that he was pointing towards a clump of coral to my right. As I looked over, I saw what was causing all the excitement: a giant sea turtle. It was amazing – this animal, so ungainly on land, floating and

swimming so gracefully in its natural environment.

At one point, when Alex and I had left the film crew (and the lights) far behind, he motioned for me to turn off my torch. With my heart in my mouth, I did as he'd asked and then he switched his off, too. With that noiseless click, the sea turned into the blackest of black ink, and I couldn't even see my hand in front of my face. In the back of my mind, all I could hear was the score from *Jaws*, and I expected that, at any moment, an enormous hungry *something* would come streaking out of the dark . . .

The lights couldn't have been switched off for more than a minute, but it seemed like an eternity, and I was relieved when Alex turned on his torch again and I followed suit. It struck me that not many people will ever experience such utter darkness, with the result that they'll never fully appreciate how wonderful the light can be.

By now, Mike had taken the film crew up on to the boat, and as Alex and I surfaced, he shouted that he wanted to film us from above, to get the glow of our torches under the water. We obliged by swimming a short distance away and then heading back towards the boat while staying fairly near the surface. However, the current was strong here and, what with the darkness, I began swimming in the wrong direction and was soon totally disorientated. I felt quite weird, and almost went limp with relief when I felt Alex's strong hand on my arm guiding me back towards the boat.

Finally, I pulled myself up the ladder and on to the deck, feeling a

Day 6 continued

real sense of achievement at having completed my first night dive without having got lost . . . or swallowed. Although I hadn't enjoyed parts of it, I was very grateful to have had the chance to do it – there aren't many occasions when you can go on a night dive in such a wonderful place and with such pros. Besides, I was lucky to have it registered in my logbook, ready for future qualifications.

A lovely supper was waiting for us, and we tucked in ravenously. As we were debating whether to have a second helping of the rhubarb crumble, we heard sounds from *outside* the boat! Looking over the port side, a strange sight came into view out of the darkness: three dark, swarthy gentlemen with broad grins, coming alongside the *Lady Jenny* in their fishing boat.

They were obviously far too friendly to be pirates, and were, in fact, bedouin fishermen, hoping to barter some of their catch for beer. This presented Adrian with an excellent opportunity to demonstrate yet another of his exceptional skills: we were *most* impressed as we listened to him bartering with our visitors in fluent Arabic.

We hung over the side as he and the bedouins completed their transaction. Then, to our amazement, one of them knelt down in the tiny boat and began to pray towards Mecca! It was a strange sight. Graham grabbed the camera and filmed them and then, inviting them aboard we played back the video. Delighted with their starring roles, they chucked us an extra couple of fish before climbing over the side and sailing away into the gloom.

I began to yawn and yawn until I was finally persuaded to call it a day

Day 6 continued

– and what a day it had been. Tomorrow would be our last day in the Red Sea, something I could hardly bear to contemplate. I almost sleepwalked my way into bed, but I was still aware of that feeling of regret that comes when a wonderful experience is almost over.

According to Aristotle, Alexander the Great went to the bottom of the sea in a diving bell where, so the philosopher says, the young conqueror saw 'underwater sheep and dogs and a great creature that took three days to pass'. (Sounds like the first documented case of nitrogen narcosis!) Despite this frightening vision, Alexander successfully used divers during the siege of Tyre in 332 BC.

The Gulf of Aqaba, the Red Sea's eastern 'arm' where we were diving, is the lower end of a large rift in the earth's crust, which once extended north through what is now the modern State of Israel. The rest of the rift's remains can still be seen from space (via satellites) as a straight line that takes in the Dead Sea and the Sea of Galilee.

DAY 7

For once, I was awake before everyone else, and enjoying the solitude. I went up on deck, making sure that I stepped carefully over the slumbering Ray. Leaning over the rail, I stared sadly at the now-docile Red Sea, which seemed as hypnotized as I was by the beauty of the peachy early-morning sun. I was filled with that strong feeling of nostalgia that comes when you know you're about to leave. Life at sea was, without doubt, an effective antidote to the stress of London life.

Well, it was no use moping on deck. I had a lot to look forward to today and wanted to make the most of it. We'd been regaled with tales of all the wrecks in these parts – a result of the treacherous coral reefs and violent storms – and although there wasn't much time left now, Alex had promised to take me down to one this morning for our first (and deepest) dive of the day.

By the time he was passing the tea-and-biscuits tray round to the others, I was already waiting

The British Sub-Aqua Club (address on page 38) has a list of Recognised Schools providing proper scuba training.

One of these is the London Underwater Centre, 13 Glendower Road, London SW14 8NY (tel: 01-876 0735), where Reg Vallintine can be found.

If you are ecologically minded, the Marine Conservation Society (4 Gloucester Rd, Ross-on-Wye, Herefordshire HR9 5BU) may be for you. They organize surveys and projects for divers interested in the conservation of the sea.

Day 7 continued

in my wet suit, impatient to get going.

'We're quite lucky with the state of the sea this morning,' Alex told me. 'It can sometimes get a bit murky when the current stirs up all the sand and plankton that collects around a wreck, but today the visibility should be quite good.'

He motioned to the other divers on deck. 'Now, everyone gather round for a moment while I tell you a little bit about this wreck. Have a look at this drawing that Adrian's made.'

We were to dive the *Dunraven*, a cargo ship built in Newcastle in 1873, which met its fate three years later at Beacon Rock, an underwater crag that just breaks the surface. At the time, the ship was miles from anywhere, but today, its grave was only a short journey from where we were anchored. Alex and Tamara started exploring it only a few years ago, and although they weren't the only divers to have discovered it, it was still relatively unplundered. (Later, Tamara told me how excited she'd been when she found a cracked dinner plate with 'DUNRAVEN' still clearly written on it. It was now displayed proudly in the *Lady Jenny*'s lounge.)

The wreck, in quite a state of decay, was lying aslant on a coral ledge. As the stern had come to rest about 30 metres down, we weren't going to have much time. Glancing at my decompression table, I calculated quickly: we could dive for 20 minutes at that depth without needing a stop.

Using Adrian's drawing, Alex showed us the gaping hole where we'd enter the ship – where the *Dunraven* had obviously come a major cropper – and then traced the journey we'd make through the main hold and boiler room. We were to pop out halfway along as the midship was blocked by debris, and then we would examine the arcaded bow section that was at a much shallower depth, sticking up at about 20 metres.

We were to dive the wreck in relays, Tamara and the French doctors going down first, with Alex and me following on later. All of us were given strict instructions to keep closely behind our dive leader and, as there were some narrow gang-

Day 7 continued

ways and dark chambers, a torch was essential. We were told to watch out for jagged edges of rusty iron and to make sure that we secured our equipment closely about us to avoid catching it on anything. We were also to beware of creatures lurking in gloomy corners – this was definitely to be a 'gloves-on' dive . . .

Exploring a wreck is the ultimate diving adventure. It didn't even matter that I wasn't the first to discover the *Dunraven*; I could practically hear the orchestra tuning up as we plunged in. I felt quite emotional actually. Reg and Graham were holding cables and lights, other divers had been roped in, too – and I found that I kept thinking, *Gulp – all this is for me!*

As we descended further and further into the depths, the marine landscape that I'd become familiar with during our days around Ras Muḥammed changed dramatically. Gradually, the brightly coloured

Always remember that almost all wrecks are owned by someone, and you can take things from them only if you obtain permission.

Wreck diving can be fascinating, and even amateur divers can work on historic wrecks – the *Mary Rose* being the most famous of recent years. Contact the Nautical Archaeology Society (Institute of Archaeology, 31–34 Gordon Sq., London WC1H 0PY) for information on how to join this association that exists for all those interested in underwater archaeology.

Day 7 continued

fish that thrived in the sunlit areas disappeared, and we entered a shadowy world, inhabited by hundreds of little glass fish that shimmered in the gloom with an effect like that of dappled light through the leaves of a tree.

It was an incredible dive. Alex and I weaved in and out of the wreckage, stopping to reflect silently on this watery 'ghost town'. At one stage, we did have a good laugh when Mike got his camera wedged in a doorway. We nearly left him there . . .

As I hauled myself up the ladder on to the deck of the *Lady Jenny* – the abrupt change in the weight of my equipment kept taking me by surprise – my senses were suddenly assaulted by the aroma of more of that fabulous French toast wafting over the side, and I was immediately enormously hungry.

Time was running out . . . we only had a few precious hours left on board. As the *Jenny* set sail back to Ras Muhammed, Tamara mysteriously produced some hard-boiled eggs and put them in a satchel that she attached to her waist. No one would tell me what they were for, and I couldn't imagine what we would do with boiled eggs in the sea! Perhaps this was part of the advanced course: eating while wearing an aqualung? I did, however, hear Tamara whisper the words 'Napoleon wrasse' to Mike – was this significant, I asked myself. It was.

Yesterday, when I'd done my 'studying' underwater, one type of fish that I'd noticed swimming around had been Napoleon wrasse. They were hard to miss: the largest species of wrasse in the world,

growing up to 2 metres long, they were, despite their beautiful green-dappled scales, exceptionally ugly with a large bump on their 'forehead' and swivelling beady eyes. (Why they were called *Napoleon* wrasse, we never did find out.)

We anchored at Ras Muhammed, and Tamara and I finned a short way from where we'd descended from the *Lady Jenny*, shadowed by the ubiquitous camera-laden Mike and Alex. Suddenly, Tamara signalled for us to stop, and she scanned the water, holding one of the eggs, hidden in her hand. She must have seen what she was looking for: as she held out the egg, a wrasse suddenly whooshed towards her, and she released it a split second before the monster snapped her hand too. I was stunned: the wrasse had seemed so enormously powerful and, for a fish of its bulk, incredibly swift and agile.

Day 7 continued

Now it was my turn. I held out an egg, and as I let it go, one of the wrasse barged in, sucked it into its wide mouth and surged past me. It was a glorious sensation – so far underwater in a beautiful coral world with huge fish eating out of my hand.

Time to try again, but now everything did *not* go to plan. I took another egg from Tamara's satchel and looked around to see where the wrasse were. I'd just spotted a male swimming towards me and was holding the egg out to him when, from above and behind me, a female – equally big and aggressive and obviously jealous at the attention I was paying to the male – hurtled down. She grabbed the egg directly from my hand and, in the process, nearly took it off, her powerful teeth peeling back my glove. My hand hurt so much that I really thought I'd lost a couple of fingers, and I looked around anxiously in case another attack was imminent.

Tamara swam to me quickly to check that I was all right, and I

Day 7 continued

turned towards Mike for some sympathy. He made a touching, caring gesture . . . you guessed it: 'Hurry up – let's do it again.' I couldn't win! Perhaps it was like remounting after being thrown by a horse – anyway, I knew that the filmed sequence that followed would be terrific, photographed as it was from two different angles, and showing in great detail the force of the wrasse as it sucked in the egg, glowing delicately in the current.

After the wrasse attack, I was more than ready to get back to the *Jenny* to attend to my wounds, but when I'd stripped off my wet suit and had my hand seen to, I felt extraordinarily alive – as if the episode with the Napoleon wrasse had been more life- than *hand*-threatening!

That should have been my last dive in the Red Sea. If I hadn't already taken off my wet suit, I swear I would have jumped back in for just one last look, one last weightless somersault, one last . . . But no, my diving days were over, at least for a while – or so I thought.

I went below to my cabin and began the laborious task of trying to make myself presentable to a non-nautical world. After battling to get all the salt off me in the impossibly tiny shower, I finally emerged on deck feeling squeaky clean, hair dried and totally salt-free. Adrian was shouting orders to his crew, in preparation for the journey back to Sharm-el-Sheikh, but even his best-laid plans didn't take into account Mike's obsession with getting 'just one more shot' . . .

I could have killed him, I really could. There I was, all dressed up *and* with somewhere to go, and here was Mike telling Reg and me to tug on our wet suits again and jump in! I didn't even raise an eyebrow though, such had been my conditioning over the last week; instead, I obediently struggled back into my soaking wet suit (have you ever tried to do this?). And giving each other our mutual 'look' of resignation – perfected over the previous six days – Reg and I plunged in. *'Ere we go, 'ere we go, 'ere we go.*

Once in, we thought we might as well make the most of it, and not caring that we were being filmed, we swam and dived for the sheer pleasure of it, imitating the dolphins we'd seen two days before, turning somersaults – simply and totally enjoying the freedom of our best dive yet. It was very special, diving with Reg again – this time as his *partner*, rather than his pupil. There was an unspoken bond between us, of having shared a unique experience.

Day 7 continued

Finally it was time to go – for real this time – and I disappeared below decks to get clean yet again. As I stepped into the shower, I heard the engine start up, and knew that we would soon be arriving at Sharm-el-Sheikh.

The omens were still good: when I got back on deck, I saw that the dolphins had returned! They accompanied us, playing gleefully all round the boat, until we neared Sharm. In fact, they were almost as difficult to say good-bye to as Alex, Tamara, Adrian and the rest of the *Lady Jenny*'s crew.

Once we'd cleared customs at the port, we loaded our gear into the minibus and, shortly after six o'clock, headed back up the long road to Eilat. Depending on the driver, it can take anything between two and four hours to reach the Taba checkpoint, which closes for

The production team hard at work

Day 7 continued

the night at 9.00 p.m. We all began to look frantically at our watches as the deadline approached – if we didn't make it in time, we'd have to camp in the middle of the desert until morning – literally! I didn't fancy that at all; since we'd left the *Lady Jenny*, I'd mentally changed gear and was dying to get back to civilization and to a good long soak in a big warm bath. But the luck of the dolphins held good, and we breathed a collective sigh of relief as we spotted the checkpoint – with only ten minutes to go . . .

Our timing was impeccable: because it was so late, both sets of customs officials, Egyptian and Israeli, rushed us through, barely searching us. It was a great improvement on the two hours we'd had to spend there on the way down, and everyone was especially friendly, perhaps because they, too, were looking forward to some creature comforts at home. To celebrate, we opened another bottle of champagne (how it had escaped the attention of our thirsty crew, I'll never know).

The King Solomon's Palace Hotel was something of a culture shock. There couldn't be anything less like life aboard the *Lady Jenny*. To us, exhausted after hours of being battered around in the minibus – not to mention the dawn start and the two dives – it was like a true oasis in the middle of that desert.

Farewell to the Lady Jenny

Day 7 continued

My hotel room seemed absolutely *huge* after my tiny cabin, but I spent very little time inspecting it, instead heading straight for the bath (I seemed to have collected most of the dust from the Sinai during our journey north). Some of my tiredness drained away as I sank into the silky water in the tub, but I still thought that there was no way that I could drag myself down to dinner; room service would be an added luxury.

But old habits die hard – after only a week, I was firmly into a team mode and couldn't imagine eating unless all seven of us were together. The dinner that night was wonderful, not because of the food, the Israeli champagne (it certainly wasn't because of *that*!) or even the classical guitarist in the corner, but because of the infectious enthusiasm that spread wildly around the table. I'd never felt quite like this after a shoot – due, perhaps, to a combination of my enthralment with the fabulous world of diving to which I'd been introduced *and* the very difficult conditions under which we had worked those long, hard seven days.

Mike's absolutely madcap determination to get it right had been very challenging, and made all of us believe totally in the project. Although he'd been an absolute slave driver, we all felt that this film was the best thing we'd ever done.

Reg said that, when he got back home, he was going to write a book entitled *Dives of less than Two Feet in Egypt*. This caused a great shout of laughter. We all remembered how Mike, to get his artistic shots of bubbles coming to the surface, had told Reg, 'Just get down there and breathe.' Reg obediently did as he was asked, and was underwater for ages because no one remembered to tell him to come up!

As we sat over our coffee, it became apparent that none of us could wait to get back to England – to see the film and talk about it and tell everybody in the world about it and show off our scars. But part of us would always be back there in the Red Sea, among the fishes and the coral, sharing a subaqueous adventure of a lifetime.

About a week after we returned to London, I invited over everyone who'd been on the shoot to see the rushes of the film Mike had shot underwater. At about midnight, we settled down in front of the television, drinks in hand, and because the soundtrack hadn't yet been added, I put some Sibelius on the stereo as background music.

For the next two hours, we sat spellbound as we relived our adventures, stunned by the beauty of the photography. Had we really been lucky enough to have seen all that ourselves? The music seemed to have been written especially for the film, uncannily reflecting what was on the screen – lyrical passages as Reg and I swam silently side by side, dramatic music as a Napoleon wrasse swam up to take an egg out of my hand. And as we all laughed hysterically when yet another film moment was counterpointed by yet more appropriate music, I felt again the great camaraderie that makes diving such a terrific sport.

I'd done about 30 dives in five days. I probably wouldn't have done as many if I hadn't been making a film, but it was all great experience. Now that I'd gained confidence in the equipment and in my ability to carry out everything I'd learned, I knew that I'd be lured back.

Thanks to Reg and Mike, I now realize that there's a lot more to diving than just learning how to use an aqualung. It's more than just a sport: it's given me the opportunity to explore a whole new world I might otherwise never have known.

Postscript

About two weeks after we got back, I finally got round to unpacking my bag of diving kit, only to be repelled by the most disgusting smell. And even though I rinsed everything in it time and time again, something still smelled absolutely terrible. Eventually, after searching every corner, I discovered, tucked away in the pocket of my 'stab' jacket, a thoroughly rotten egg – one that had been intended for the Napoleon wrasse. It was my only memento of that exciting day!